On Order, Authority, and Modern Civil-Military Relations

READING AUGUSTINE

Series Editor
Miles Hollingworth
In collaboration with the Wessel-Hollingworth Foundation

Reading Augustine presents books that offer personal, nuanced and oftentimes literary readings of Saint Augustine of Hippo. Each time, the idea is to treat Augustine as a spiritual and intellectual icon of the Western tradition, and to read through him to some or other pressing concern of our current day, or to some enduring issue or theme. In this way, the writers follow the model of Augustine himself, who produced his famous output of words and ideas in active tussle with the world in which he lived. When the series launched, this approach could raise eyebrows, but now that technology and pandemics have brought us into the world and society like never before, and when scholarship is expected to live the same way and responsibly, the series is well-set and thriving.

Volumes in the series

On Creativity, Liberty, Love and the Beauty of the Law, Todd Breyfogle

On Love, Confession, Surrender and the Moral Self, Ian Clausen

On Education, Formation, Citizenship and the Lost Purpose of Learning, Joseph Clair

On Ethics, Politics and Psychology in the Twenty-First Century, John Rist

On Consumer Culture, Identity, the Church and the Rhetorics of Delight, Mark Clavier

On God, The Soul, Evil and the Rise of Christianity, John Peter Kenney

On Music, Sense, Affect, and Voice, Carol Harrison

On Solitude, Conscience, Love and Our Inner, and Outer Lives, Ron Haflidson

On Creation, Science, Disenchantment, and the Contours of Being and Knowing, Matthew W. Knotts

On Agamben, Arendt, Christianity, and the Dark Arts of Civilization, Peter Iver Kaufman

On Self-Harm, Narcissism, Atonement, and the Vulnerable Christ, David Vincent Meconi

On Faith, Works, Eternity, and the Creatures We Are, André Barbera
On Time, Change, History, and Conversion, Sean Hannan
On Compassion, Healing, Suffering, and the Purpose of the Emotional Life, Susan Wessel
On Agamben, Donatism, Pelagianism, and the Missing Links, Peter Iver Kaufman
On Memory, Marriage, Tears, and Meditation, Margaret R. Miles
On King Lear, The Confessions, and Human Experience and Nature, Kim Paffenroth
On Mystery, Ineffability, Silence, and Musical Symbolism, Laurence Wuidar
On Distance, Belonging, Isolation and the Quarantined Church of Today, Laurence Wuidar
On Images, Visual Culture, Memory and the Play without a Script, Matthias Smalbrugge
On Signs, Christ, Truth and the Interpretation of Scripture, Sussanah Ticciati
On Christology, Anthropology, Cognitive Science and the Human Body, Martin Claes
On The Confessions as 'confessio', Barry A. David
On Regular Life, Freedom, Modernity, and Augustinian Communitarianism, Guillermo M. Jodra
On Hellenism, Judaism, Individualism, and Early Christian Theories of the Subject, Guillermo M. Jodra
On the Nature, Limits, Meaning, and End of Work, Zachary Thomas Settle
On Interrogation, Introspection, Dialectic and the Ineluctable Polarity of Being and Knowing, Matthew W. Knotts

On Order, Authority, and Modern Civil-Military Relations

Lindsay P. Cohn

BLOOMSBURY ACADEMIC
LONDON • NEW YORK • OXFORD • NEW DELHI • SYDNEY

BLOOMSBURY ACADEMIC

Bloomsbury Publishing Plc, 50 Bedford Square, London, WC1B 3DP, UK
Bloomsbury Publishing Inc, 1385 Broadway, New York, NY 10018, USA
Bloomsbury Publishing Ireland, 29 Earlsfort Terrace, Dublin 2, D02 AY28, Ireland

BLOOMSBURY, BLOOMSBURY ACADEMIC and the Diana logo are trademarks of Bloomsbury Publishing Plc

First published in Great Britain 2025

Copyright © Lindsay P. Cohn, 2025

Lindsay P. Cohn has asserted her right under the Copyright, Designs and Patents Act, 1988, to be identified as Author of this work.

For legal purposes the Acknowledgments on p. ix constitute an extension of this copyright page.

Cover image: Looking Glass/Getty

All rights reserved. No part of this publication may be: i) reproduced or transmitted in any form, electronic or mechanical, including photocopying, recording or by means of any information storage or retrieval system without prior permission in writing from the publishers; or ii) used or reproduced in any way for the training, development or operation of artificial intelligence (AI) technologies, including generative AI technologies. The rights holders expressly reserve this publication from the text and data mining exception as per Article 4(3) of the Digital Single Market Directive (EU) 2019/790.

Bloomsbury Publishing Inc does not have any control over, or responsibility for, any third-party websites referred to or in this book. All internet addresses given in this book were correct at the time of going to press. The author and publisher regret any inconvenience caused if addresses have changed or sites have ceased to exist, but can accept no responsibility for any such changes.

A catalogue record for this book is available from the British Library.

A catalog record for this book is available from the Library of Congress.

ISBN: HB: 978-1-3502-9722-7
PB: 978-1-3502-9721-0
ePDF: 978-1-3502-9723-4
ePUB: 978-1-3502-9724-1

Series: Reading Augustine

Typeset by Newgen KnowledgeWorks Pvt. Ltd., Chennai, India
Printed and bound in Great Britain

For product safety related questions contact productsafety@bloomsbury.com.

To find out more about our authors and books visit www.bloomsbury.com and sign up for our newsletters.

CONTENTS

Preface viii
Acknowledgments ix

1 Introduction: Why Augustine and Civil-Military Relations? 1

2 Order and Authority: Augustine's Highest Political Values 9

3 Liberty, Commonweal, Legitimacy, Plurality: Democracy's Highest Political Values 27

4 Militaries and Democratic Breakdown 49

5 A Democratic Military Professionalism? 71

6 Conclusion 89

References 93
Index 103

PREFACE

This book grew out of a few different strands of inquiry, which met and muddled in me. The most immediate was the turmoil in my main field of study, civil-military relations, over the crumbling of old models and the search for new ones. Broader was my long-standing interest in the question of how societies and individuals justify and legitimate the use of force or violence[1]—particularly lethal force. Deeper and older was my long questioning of how Christianity and Christian faith and beliefs related to the problem of governance, especially issues of democratic or self-governance, and those questions of legitimation of force or violence. In many ways, this book is my way of working through these problems for myself.

When I was approached with the prospect of writing about how Augustine's thought and writing might illuminate aspects of civil-military relations, I demurred, as someone who was by no means an Augustine scholar. But as the purpose of this series was explained to me—for those who are experts in something else to encounter Augustine and listen to what he says, in the hopes of finding something new and interesting about one's own field as well as bringing a new perspective to Augustine himself, it appealed to me more and more. I am not an Augustine scholar, nor am I a trained philosopher, nor an expert on democratic theory. I am a scholar of civil-military relations, who knows very little about even that, much less everything else. But I hope that readers will take this book for what it is: not the explanation or exegesis of an expert in all these things but the poor attempts at synthesis of someone who looks to these fields for help in her own.

---

[1] I appreciate Schelling's (1966) distinction between force and violence, and mean to include both in my discussions in this volume. Thus I will usually refer to "force or violence" rather than simply one or the other.

ACKNOWLEDGMENTS

I am grateful to Miles Hollingworth for giving me this opportunity, and to my friends, family, and colleagues for listening to me rattle on about it for the last three years. I apologize to all the scholars whose work I failed to engage or engaged with less depth than they deserved. This book was very much a solitary venture, so any mistakes, oversights, or misinterpretations lie with me alone.

1

Introduction: Why Augustine and Civil-Military Relations?

For many years, scholars of civil-military relations have been dissatisfied with the model of professionalism and the professional military ethic we inherited from Samuel Huntington in 1957 (Cohen 2002; Brooks 2020). This concern gained very practical urgency with the US presidency of Donald Trump, which raised a number of questions for both practitioners and scholars about how to reconcile the demands of professional obligation, personal morality, and belief in democracy. Being asked to write this book offered an opportunity for me to dig through Augustine's moral and ethical thoughts about war, society, and authority, to see if it would help to shed any light on these dilemmas.

As I note in the preface, I am neither an Augustine scholar nor a philosopher of ethics or of democracy, and I do not make any claim to be resolving these great questions with the erudition of any of those specialists. I am merely a political scientist who studies civil-military relations, looking to these fields for perspective and possibly some clarity.

The Problems

Civil-Military Relations

The first problem, as mentioned above, is the current churn in the field of civil-military relations, provoked by a growing recognition that the classical Western concept of military professionalism is inadequate to today's political problems (if, indeed, it was ever adequate). The specific political problems in question are the tensions between values of pluralistic democracy and those of nationalism, autocracy, and/or populism. These tensions are of course not new, but two specific waves of political phenomena have focused public and scholarly attention on the civil-military implications. The first was the Arab Spring, from 2010 to around 2013–14, in which popular uprisings challenged autocratic governments with demands for more political rights and voice. In every one of these uprisings, the government attempted to respond with some level of military repression (though some also sought to conciliate the protestors with concessions). In every one of these cases, military personnel had to decide how to respond to those orders. Should they fire on simple citizens demanding freedom and rights? Should they join the protestors and overthrow the government? Should they refuse to engage at all (Bellin 2012; Pion-Berlin, Esparza, and Grisham 2014; Albrecht and Ohl 2016)?

These situations raised serious questions for long-accepted Western norms of civil-military relations, such as the principle of obedience to the duly constituted political authority. In the classic view, the military professional was meant to view him/herself as a political instrument, subject entirely to the decision-making rules of that polity, not as a judge of policy. The only exception to this was supposed to be manifestly illegal orders. But the Arab Spring emphasized the point that legality and legitimacy are not the same thing, and when the Tunisian military refused to suppress the protesters with force, they were felt to be doing right. And when the Egyptian military helped to oust Mubarak, Western commentators found themselves unable to think it was the wrong thing to do, under the circumstances.

For the most part, scholars and pundits managed to square this circle to themselves by saying that autocratic regimes were simply less legitimate than democratic regimes, and thus it was theoretically possible for a military professional to recognize that some orders from autocrats, while legal, were not legitimate because they violated universal human rights. This narrative, however, became seriously challenged with the political rise of Donald Trump in the United States. Trump violated countless norms of democratic governance and civil-military relations, and the US public, rather than uniting in condemnation of those violations, split along mostly partisan lines. On the one hand, this raised the question of how deeply held those norms were in the first place (Krebs, Ralston, and Rapport 2023). On the other, it brought the questions of the Arab Spring home to a supposedly consolidated democracy: if a democratically elected, and therefore fully procedurally legitimate, leader, supported by democratic institutions such as Congress and the Supreme Court, ordered the forcible repression of certain groups, or activities, in ways that seemed illegitimate, wrong, or unconstitutional, what was the member of the armed forces to do? Classical civil-military relations theory and military professional ethics said "obey." But for many citizens and service-members, the idea seemed repulsive. This situation created new impetus in both the empirical study of democratic breakdown or backsliding and the philosophical study of what democratic governance actually is—what is essential to its nature and what is not; what are the sources of legitimacy; and how do we identify the transition from legitimate to illegitimate.

It also created momentum in the field of civil-military relations to revisit those classical models of professional ethics. Not that they had not been continually questioned already, but criticism now began to build to a critical mass. The embodiment of the classical model was Huntington's 1957 book, *The Soldier and the State*. There, he laid out what he saw as the central problem of civil-military relations: how a democratic society with a liberal constitution (like the United States) could have a military that was both capable of defeating a major military rival (the Soviet Union) and totally subordinate to civilian (democratic) political control. His solution was a particular concept of professionalism for the military officer, in which the officer focused on becoming an expert at his core technical task (being better at winning a conventional great power war than any rival) and the civilian policymakers refrained from interfering with the officer within that sphere of competency. In theory, this was supposed to socialize officers to think and care only about their own technical expertise, accepting all policy or "political" questions as far outside their sphere of competence. This would cause them to refrain voluntarily from interference in policymaking or politics writ large, achieving the goal of preventing the military from preying on society. At the same time, if the policymakers respected the military officer's sphere of expertise and refrained from interfering with them, that would also achieve the other goal of having a highly competent and effective military. This approach had the added bonus, according to Huntington, of being safe and appropriate for democratically constituted polities, as it meant the military officer would be so "politically sterile" that he would serve whatever legitimate government was in power, even if his own personal political affinities lay with another party. Moreover, it relied on principles of meritocracy and technical competence for selection and promotion, rather than political considerations, further improving the likely effectiveness of the armed forces (see also Talmadge 2015).

This all sounds excellent, and indeed, most Anglo-, Franco-, and Germanophone societies (and those subjected to their colonial rule) have tended to adopt this model of military professionalism (Fitch 1998).[1] It also carries echoes of earlier philosophical concepts of how to achieve both control and military excellence, including in the work of Plato (*The Republic*) and other classical writers. But Huntington's view was not hegemonic when he wrote it, and while it has dominated Western military thought since the 1950s, a steady stream of criticism has now mounted to a roar that may shake him from his pedestal (Brooks 2020).

Main critiques of the Huntington model can be summarized under five headings: the (potentially increasing) difficulty of actually distinguishing between "the military" and "the political" such that military professionals can focus exclusively on the former and ignore the latter (Sarkesian 1981; Cohn 2018; Brooks 2020); the problems in strategic planning and military effectiveness that result from a military neither competent in political issues nor willing to talk them through with policymakers (Sarkesian 1981;

---

[1] Note that Spain, Portugal, and the countries of Central and Latin America have had some alternative views of military professionalism—see Fitch (1998) for a detailed accounting.

Cohen 2002; Brooks 2020); the insufficiency of an ethic alone to maintain military subordination (Stepan 1988; Fitch 1998; Feaver 2003); the inevitable politicization of any group that sees itself as a corporate profession (Fitch 1998; Brooks 2020); and most recently, the inability of a military drawn from society to escape whatever issues that society is politicizing, particularly in more polarized or divided societies (Robinson, Cohn, and Margulies 2021).

At this point, there is enough criticism of the Huntington model that many scholars and even officers are willing to jettison it, but the problem is that there is no clear attractive alternative. The approach that autocratic regimes often use, of stacking the officer corps with loyalists, whether ethnic, religious, linguistic, family, or ideological (Nordlinger 1977; Quinlivan 1999), is unsuited to a democratic polity. One of the basic characteristics of democracy is that the party in power *can* lose (Przeworski 1991: 10), so having the military be loyal to one particular party or social group would be utterly inappropriate. It would also involve changing all the senior officers every time a new administration came into office, and would interfere significantly with ideas of selection and promotion on merit and competency, thus undermining military effectiveness. Another approach, taken by many Latin American states and called the "developmental" model (Fitch 1998) involves the military taking on many roles in society aside from just territorial/conventional defense. These roles can include economic and social developmental activities, meaning the military will be deeply engaged in activities that are unambiguously political. Here, the military competency is not about "managing violence," as in the Huntingtonian model, but in managing all kinds of activities, and there is significant overlap between the military and political spheres. Such a model may be culturally appropriate in some societies but requires extremely strong democratic institutions and civilian governance to keep the military in check (Fitch 1998).

And this is precisely the problem that was brought to the fore by Mr. Trump's political career: What is the military officer to do when democratic institutions themselves are in question?

One goal of this book will be to think through what an alternative professional military ethic might look like. Can we have, not a politically neutral officer, but one committed to democratic governance?

Legitimizing Force or Violence

The second big question this book hopes to explore is about how states (including both societies and governments) legitimize or justify their use of coercive—sometimes lethal—force.[2] This question applies both internally and externally, and is logically (though not necessarily historically) prior to all the questions in my field of civil-military relations. What communal values rank high enough to outweigh the individual's freedom from coercion? What constitutes the legitimacy of punishment? What determines guilt or innocence? What justifies large-scale organized violence against other groups of people? Is the individual soldier justified in killing simply because his society told him to do it?

This is far too large a topic to address even in summary form in this project. But it is critical to bring up even if truncated, because it is the source of what are called role beliefs—the beliefs held by the public and the military about what the military's role is in society and what actions are appropriate and inappropriate (Fitch 1998). No professional ethic can take seed if it is not congruent with the society's beliefs about the legitimate use of force or violence.

Augustine is widely considered to be part of the intellectual history of the Christian doctrine of Just War—the set of ideas that determine when and whether it is legitimate for a political leader to send his or her own people (whether subjects or citizens) to kill and be killed by the people of some other political leader. It is unlikely that Augustine actually viewed himself as creating such a doctrine (Wynn 2013), but it is undeniable that those who did self-consciously formulate what became known as Just War Theory (mainly Aquinas) attributed much of their thinking to Augustine (Wynn 2013; Langan 1984: 33). Indeed, given the quantity of his writings, the breadth of his subjects, and the influence he had on those medieval philosophers whose arguments shaped Western Christian political thinking for the next several centuries, it is fair to take Augustine as a jumping-off point for a discussion about how political violence can be legitimized.

---

[2]While I use the word "state" throughout this study, I do not mean to imply that all polities in history—even just European history—have been what we now think of as "states." It's simply a term of convenience to refer to politically organized societies and particularly their rules/laws and governments.

It may be particularly helpful to think about Augustine's teachings in this area as a base from which to venture out into how a largely secular, pluralistic vision of democracy might need different justifications for political violence, and how military personnel in democracies might need to think of themselves as something other than just soldiers.

Democracy

The fundamental premises of (liberal) democracy are deceptively simple: that the individual is sovereign over him/herself, and that the governed should have a voice in the rules by which they are governed. But the Devil is in the details. As we will see, there are not only multiple versions of democratic theory, but there is a tension at the very heart of the concept. Specifically: Is democracy legitimate and desirable because the processes are inherently legitimate and desirable, or are democratic processes legitimate and desirable primarily because they are believed to be most reliable at safeguarding certain values or outcomes? Should "the people" get whatever they want? Which people? These may seem like very abstract questions, but they become concrete quickly when a military officer is asked to decide whether to protect the government, the people, or some concept of "the system."

Plan of the Book

I begin with an attempt to understand how Augustine might have answered some of these questions: What is the highest political/societal value? How is the authority's use of force or violence legitimized? What is the role of the soldier or other wielder of state-sanctioned force in society? How does one reconcile a conflict of conscience and authority?

The second chapter begins from the observation that Augustine's political thought was embedded in a context very different from what the citizen of a modern democracy—particularly a liberal democracy—would expect. Given that, how would the prescriptions of democratic and liberal theory differ from those of Augustine? How do these theories conceptualize the highest political good?

How is the authority's use of force or violence legitimized? And so forth.

The third chapter recognizes that the diversity, fragmentation, and internal tensions of democratic and liberal theory cannot yield a single clear prescription for a military professional ethic, so it turns to the normative and empirical civil-military relations literature for clues. What roles do militaries play in governmental breakdown generally and democratic backsliding/breakdown more specifically? Is their role ever constructive? Can we determine a list of behaviors or values that militaries in democracies should or should not adopt?

Finally, we attempt to synthesize the lessons of Augustine, democratic and liberal theory, and empirical studies of militaries in governmental breakdown: Is there a better professional ethic available? Can military personnel be socialized specifically to defend liberal democratic governance? Or, is Huntingtonian political sterility the best we can do?

2

Order and Authority: Augustine's Highest Political Values

It is clear even to a novice reading Augustine that he is not consciously developing a political theory. In that sense, it seems almost unfair to critique his political ideas and concepts, but I am going to try to do so, anyway.

Augustine's writings were generally written either in his pastoral character, or in his apologetic character (Wynn 2013; Dyson 1998: xv). He argues consistently that the intention and the will of the individual are what matter in whether a deed is righteous or sinful, not the nature of the deed itself (see esp. *De Natura Boni, De Libero Arbitrio, Contra Faustum, De Mendacio,* and *De Civitate Dei*).[1] His writings are nearly silent on what people could or should do to make their entire society more just; they are enjoined primarily to make themselves just. When, in his discussion of the Sermon on the Mount (*De Sermone Domini Monte*), he gets to the peacemakers, there is no mention at all of making peace between nations or even among one's fellow humans; it is interpreted entirely as creating a state of peace within oneself: "the contemplation of the truth, tranquillizing the whole man, and assuming the likeness

---

[1] For example, in *Contra Faustum* XXII.73, he says: "The act, the agent, and the authority for the action are all of great importance in the order of nature. For Abraham to sacrifice his son of his own accord is shocking madness. His doing so at the command of God proves him faithful and submissive."

of God" (3.10) and "Wisdom corresponds to the peacemakers, in whom all things are now brought into order, and no passion is in a state of rebellion against reason, but all things together obey the spirit of man, while he himself also obeys God" (4.11). He is not, like Machiavelli, writing to rulers about how to rule, but to individual humans about how to reach God (cf. Langan 1984: 25).

It can be frustrating to read Augustine's works. He is sometimes inconsistent in applying principles to other gods as he does to his own God, and one can definitely see the influence of his Sophist days in his often questionable logic. But there are some ways in which he is admirably consistent, and one of them is in his insistence that the things that happen to our earthly bodies and in our earthly lives are simply not very important (see esp. *De Mendacio* and *De Civitate Dei*).[2] In *De Civitate Dei*, Augustine gives countless examples of both the good and the evil suffering and argues that, when the good suffer, it is for their edification, and when the evil suffer, it is for their punishment. Either way, the suffering comes from God and is not something to be avoided or considered unjust, because God is always just.[3]

---

[2] In *De Mendacio* (Section 9), he says:

> For that death which men are foolishly afraid of who are not afraid to sin, kills not the soul but the body, as the Lord teaches in the Gospel; whence He charges us not to fear that death: but the mouth which lies kills not the body but the soul. For in these words it is most plainly written, The mouth that lies slays the soul. How then can it be said without the greatest perverseness, that to the end one man may have life of the body, it is another man's duty to incur death of the soul? The love of our neighbor has its bounds in each man's love of himself. You shall love, says He, your neighbor as yourself. How can a man be said to love as himself that man, for whom that he may secure a temporal life, himself loses life eternal? Since if for his temporal life he lose but his own temporal life, that is not to love as himself, but more than himself: which exceeds the rule of sound doctrine. Much less then is he by telling a lie to lose his own eternal for another's temporal life. His own temporal life, of course, for his neighbor's eternal life a Christian man will not hesitate to lose: for this example has gone before, that the Lord died for us

and towards the end, "among good things chastity of mind is greater than pudicity of body; and among evil things, that which ourselves do [is worse than], than that which we suffer to be done" (Section 42).

[3] On this point, see also *De Natura Boni* (Ch. 32), where he says, "Likewise because the power even of those that are hurtful is from God alone, thus it stands written, Wisdom speaking: "Through me kings reign and tyrants hold the land through

The Highest Value

Augustine does explain what he thinks is the highest good, and calls it variably peace or happiness, by which he means a right ordering of everything, and for the human being, an endless contemplation of the loveliness of God (*The City of God*, esp. Book XIX). To achieve this goal, the human in this earthly life must focus all of his or her efforts on loving God and having a good (that is a righteous) will in all that they do. Parents should certainly correct their own children, husbands their wives, and masters their servants, in an attempt to keep those people on a path of righteousness, but Augustine does not seem to think that the role of the earthly city (or polity) is to force all of its inhabitants into Christianity or righteousness.[4] He notes that the earthly city seeks earthly peace and happiness, which are not the same as peace and happiness among the godly. For the earthly, peace is always temporary and imperfect and consists primarily of all the various parts of something (a person, a household, a polity, international society) being rightly ordered with respect to one another. Right ordering means the (naturally) lower is subjected to the (naturally) higher—so the body is subjected to

---

me" (Prov. 8:15). The apostle also says: "For there is no power but of God" (Rom. 13:1). But that it is worthily done is written in the book of Job: "Who makes to reign a man that is a hypocrite, on account of the perversity of the people." And concerning the people of Israel, God says: "I gave them a king in my wrath" (Hos. 13:11). For it is not unrighteous, that the wicked receiving the power of being hurtful, both the patience of the good should be proved and the iniquity of the evil punished. For through power given to the Devil both Job was proved so that he might appear righteous, and Peter was tempted lest he should be presumptuous, and Paul was buffeted lest he should be exalted (2 Cor. 12:7), and Judas was damned so that he should hang himself (Mt. 27:5). When, therefore, through the power which He has given the Devil, God Himself shall have done all things righteously, nevertheless punishment shall at last be rendered to the Devil not for these things justly done, but for the unrighteous willing to be hurtful, which belonged to himself, when it shall be said to the impious who persevered in consenting to his wickedness, "Go into everlasting fire which my God has prepared for the Devil and his angels" (Mt. 25:41). See also *Contra Faustum* XXII.72, where Augustine counters Faustus's argument that a righteous God would never have ordered the Hebrews to despoil the Egyptians as they fled Egypt, by arguing that "such a command can be rightly given by no other than the true and good God, who alone knows the suitable command in every case, and who alone is incapable of inflicting unmerited suffering on any one."
[4] Though late in his life he did think the government had a role in punishing heretics.

the soul; the children, women, and servants subjected to the head of household; the citizens subjected to the ruler(s) and the laws; and the worse nations subjected to the better (*De Civitate Dei* and *De Mendacio*).[5] However, when there is disagreement among the parts—for example, when those subjected to another's authority rebel or resist that authority—then peace is shattered. Augustine makes it very clear that true peace and happiness are impossible in this earthly existence, precisely because humans are sinful and some of them will inevitably do wicked things. There is no social or political organization that is "good" in the Platonic sense or that will create lasting peace or order. Rulers ought to rule well because all people ought to do whatever they do with a righteous will and with a view to serving God, but whether a people is ruled well or badly is something the people are simply supposed to accept, not try to change.

This, then, is the source of Augustine's view of politics, to the extent that he has one: the highest political good is order, and order is hierarchical. Augustine is not claiming that earthly rulers ought to aim at order or peace—again, he does not think that any person ought to aim at anything but serving God and doing right—but he does think that doing right, in the office of a ruler, consists of making good laws, punishing the wrongdoer, and generally achieving and maintaining peace and proper order among the citizens.[6]

It is from the primacy of order that we understand why authority plays such an important role in Augustine's discussions of civil servants and soldiers. The argument goes like this: power/authority

---

[5]In *De Mendacio*, for example, he says: "For chastity of mind is, love well ordered, which does not place the greater below the smaller."
[6]In *De Ordine*, a much earlier writing, Augustine argues that order came into existence only with the emergence of evil (because order is the giving of everything its due, and dues can be different only if some things are good and some are evil). I consider this non-credible, because there are clearly orders that have nothing to do with better and worse: for example, harmony is clearly ordered, but its order does not consist of separating the bad from the good, but of arranging things good in themselves (notes, melodies) into an even greater whole, producing complex beauty from simple beauty. Thus order is not something that arose only once evil existed and to clearly distinguish the evil from the good (why would we need order to do so?), and evil is not a necessary component of order. In *The City of God*, Augustine does not make this argument, so it is possible that he altered his thinking over time. That being said, he still thinks that order is about placing the better in charge of the worse, so at least in the earthly city, order is necessarily hierarchical.

is given by God. If the government/ruler is good, the people under it should be grateful to God for the blessing and strive to be virtuous. If the government/ruler is bad, the people under it should be grateful to God for the lesson and strive to be virtuous. The people are not in a position to understand why God has placed this person or persons in authority, only to accept that He has, and that their place in society—their place in the order—is to obey the authorities placed over them.

By the same token, those serving the government directly have even less room to question its policies or their orders. They have been placed by God in a different role, and if they seek to do right, they will accept the orders given them and carry them out as well as they can with a righteous will.

Legitimizing Violence

One of Augustine's recurring points is that God's plan is a mystery that cannot be fully known or understood by humans in this earthly existence. We must simply have faith that God is good, just, and in control and believe that anything that seems unjust or wrong is something God either caused to happen for good reason, or something he allowed wicked man to do for good reason (*De Ordine, De Quanitate Animae, Civitate Dei,* and *De Natura Boni*).[7]

---

[7] The argument in *De Ordine* is that the Godly order of things is knowable only to God and to the select few who dedicate their lives to learning and thinking and living the proper way; everyone else is unable to see the true pattern and thus never understands exactly what the purpose is of any given situation; they must therefore rely on authority, not on their own reason. Moreover, obedience to authority comes before and is necessary to understanding of the greater pattern. Ignorance can be overcome only by docility in the face of authority until one has attained true wisdom. In *De Quanitate Animae*, he says,

> For he (God) has judged it to be the height of excellence that everything that exists be precisely as it is; that there be such order in a graded arrangement of nature that when we consider the whole universe no flaw of any kind should offend our sensibilities; and that every punishment and every reward of the soul should always make some contribution measuring up to the beauty and order proper to all things. The soul ... has received free will ... [and] the gift of free will is such that no matter what the soul undertakes with it, it does not disturb any part of the divine order and law ... But to see these things as they should be seen is given to only a few, and no one is rendered fit for this except by true religion. (110)

Therefore, since God is the sole source of earthly authority, even if you are a soldier in the service of a wicked ruler, you must still obey that ruler, and do so with a good will, because God is using that ruler (and you) to fulfill His ultimate plan.[8]

Augustine states explicitly that killing people in the capacity of soldier or executioner under the law is not sinful killing (*Contra*

In *De Natura Boni*, he says,

> Accordingly, if all natures should guard their own proper measure and form and order, there would be no evil: but if any one should wish to misuse these good things, not even thus does he vanquish the will of God, who knows how to order righteously even the unrighteous; so that if they themselves through the iniquity of their will should misuse His good things, He through the righteousness of His power may use their evil deeds, rightly ordaining to punishment those who have perversely ordained themselves to sins. (Ch. 37)

[8] Augustine makes a similar point in *De Mendacio*, that it is more important to avoid sinning, oneself, than to try to avert or correct for another's sin:

> One must conclude then that the sins of others, be they what they may, those always excepted which defile him on whom they are committed, a man must not seek to avoid by sin of his own, either for himself or for any other, but rather he must put up with them, and suffer bravely; and if by no sins of his own he ought to avoid them, therefore not by a lie: but those which by being committed upon a man do make him unclean, these we are bound to avoid even by sinning ourselves; and for this reason those things are not to be called sins, which are done for the purpose of avoiding that uncleanness. For whatever is done, in consideration that the not doing it were just cause of blame, that thing is not sin. Upon the same principle, neither is that to be called uncleanness when there is no way of avoiding it; for even in that extremity he who suffers it has what he may do aright, namely, patiently bear what he cannot avoid. Now no man while acting aright can be defiled by any corporal contagion. For the unclean in the sight of God is every one who is unrighteous; clean therefore is every one who is righteous; if not in the sight of men, yet in the sight of God, Who judges without error. Nay, even in the act of suffering that defilement with power given of avoiding it, it is not by the mere contact that the man is defiled; but by the sin of refusing to avoid it when he might. For that would be no sin, whatever might be done for the avoiding of it. Whoever therefore, for the avoiding of it, shall tell a lie, sins not.

It is important to note, however, that Augustine contradicts himself multiple times in *De Mendacio*, in some cases arguing that one may sin to avoid the kind of sin committed against one by others that defile one, but other times gives the same example (e.g., being used carnally) as the type of thing one ought *not* to lie to avoid. Here again, he also encounters the problem that he thinks killing is not sinful when ordered by authority, but lying would be. He also makes this point more briefly in *Contra Faustum* XXII.20.

Adimantum, De Mendacio, and *Civitate Dei*).[9] He makes this point particularly starkly in *Contra Faustum*, when he says,

> for in wars carried on by divine command, [Moses] showed not ferocity but obedience; and God in giving the command, acted not in cruelty, but in righteous retribution, giving to all what they deserved, and warning those who needed warning. What is the evil in war? Is it the death of some who will soon die in any case, that others may live in peaceful subjection? This is mere cowardly dislike, not any religious feeling. The real evils in war are love of violence, revengeful cruelty, fierce and implacable enmity, wild resistance, and the lust of power, and such like. (Section 74)

Here we see again the main premises of Augustine's thinking: the evil of a deed is in the will (or passions) of the doer, not in the deed; a deed that would seem horrible if done according to human will is perfectly acceptable if done according to God's command; humans cannot know God's plan, and therefore cannot judge the justice of a command of God, or even of things that happen to them without knowing whether they were commanded by God or not; and what happens to the body—torture, rape, violence, death—is simply not as important as what happens within the soul (Langan 1984: 25).

Indeed, there is some killing that is technically sinful because it is not sanctioned by lawful authority but is nonetheless not the worst kind of sinful as it is done for understandable reasons and indicative of vigor. In *Contra Faustum* XXII.70, Augustine has a discussion of Moses slaying the Egyptian, Paul persecuting the church, and Peter cutting off the servant's ear, and he essentially says these were not righteous killings/uses of violence, because they are not sanctioned by authority (though Paul's violence was in fact sanctioned by authority), but that these were not sins unto death because they resulted from vigorous habits of mind that were as yet

---

[9] In *De Mendacio* (Section 23), he says,

> What, is this the case with what is set down there, You shall not kill? If this be in every sort evil, how shall one clear of this crime even just men, who, upon a law given, have killed many? But, it is rejoined, that man does not himself kill, who is the minister of some just command. These men's fear, then, I do accept, that I still think that laudable man who would neither lie, nor betray a man, did both better understand that which is written, and what he understood did bravely put in practice.

not appropriately cultivated by faith in and obedience to God. He says, "Here was evil [the killing/violence] to be subdued or rooted out; but the heart with such capacities needed only, like good soil, to be cultivated to make it fruitful in virtue."

Because of these premises, it is not entirely clear how Augustine would have answered the question of "unlawful orders." What ought a soldier or civil servant to do when ordered by a rightful authority to do something manifestly against the law? On the one hand, the authority going against his own laws would seem to be a situation in which the soldier or civil servant should prioritize general order rather than authority and refuse the command. On the other hand, if all authority comes from God and is turned via His mysterious plan toward the good, should not the soldier or civil servant obey the authority over him? In *De Ordine*, Augustine says, "authority is partly divine and partly human"—divine authority is "true, firm, and supreme" but can be imitated by the Devil and the good person must be on the lookout for such deception. He does not, however, explain how the good person is to know the difference. Presumably only as a result of long mental and spiritual discipline.

One of the biggest difficulties with this part of Augustine's thought, though, is that he is very clear in multiple writings that earthly authority and order are absolutely not to be considered by the Christian as overriding God's law to them. So, for example, if earthly law requires one to worship idols, the Christian is bound to refuse this authority and rebel against this order (and docilely accept the punishment for doing so). But it is never clear why earthly authority allows the Christian to violate some commandments (thou shalt not kill), but not others (thou shalt have no other Gods before me; thou shalt not bear false witness).[10] Thus the Augustinian soldier might be forgiven for wondering whether he was to obey an order to torture someone who appeared to him to be innocent and not taking part in combat. There is no clear guide here.

Indeed, the question of legitimate authority does not appear at all. One who is in a position of authority may have gotten there by good means or by evil, and may rule or command righteously

---

[10]On the point of lying, in *De Mendacio*, Augustine argues that there is never any justification for a Christian to lie, even to save a life, though the Christian may go so far as to withhold information.

or sinfully, but the question of whether that person ought to have authority is answered bluntly by the scriptural assertion that all authority comes from God.

As mentioned in the introduction, Augustine's thought is considered part of the tradition of Just War theory—the notion that wars are legitimate if they are initiated due to a just cause, as a last resort, by a legitimate authority, with the proper intent (cf. Augustine's "good will"), with means proportional to ends, and with a reasonable chance of success (e.g., Langan 1984; Walzer 2002; Crawford 2003: 6–7). Certainly, Augustine thinks that good rulers can fight wars, indicating that he thinks that collective organized violence is sometimes justified in the earthly city's terms and not contrary to the terms of the city of God. But the only aspects of just war theory that he discusses explicitly are the just cause and the proper intent. Indeed, in Augustine's eyes, the authority is always legitimate, and his understanding of the legitimacy of punishment for evil would indicate that war need not be a last resort if it is the appropriate action. Even the idea of just cause was already present in pre-Christian thinking about war, as was the idea of proportionality (Langan 1984: 20).

We may summarize like this:

- There is nothing morally wrong with joining the military or becoming a soldier; this is demonstrated by the accounts in Scripture where soldiers have asked what they should do, and are never told to lay down arms (*Contra Faustum* and *Letter to Boniface*).
- Soldiers must obey the orders of their superiors, who are exercising legitimate authority by virtue of the fact that they are where they are.
- This is true even for actions that would otherwise be considered horrific or immoral, because God works through authority toward His ultimate just plan, and because things done out of obedience and without ill will or passion are not actually evil.
- It is not clear what a soldier ought to do in the case of an order that clearly contradicts an earthly law.
- It is not clear which of God's commandments can be broken because ordered by authority, and which should be upheld even to martyrdom.

This makes it clear that the only thing a soldier needs to justify violence or lethal force is an order from someone in their chain of command and an absence of passion or enjoyment in the killing. There is no other set of criteria to which the soldier may appeal against the order.

And as for how the state justifies the use of violence or lethal force, Augustine's view is primarily one of punishment in the pursuit of order. Within the polity, those who break the laws not only can, but should, be punished (although authorities have discretion about whether they think mercy would be more effective than punishment in any given case). Outside the polity, force can be justified to punish the wrongdoing of another polity, or to defend the polity from attack. However, even if the polity is engaging in illegitimate violence, the soldier may not on that account refuse their orders.

It is important to emphasize that this view of things not only discounts any role for the individual's conscience but biases individual action toward violent action, as both Augustine's theory of punishment and his theory of order indicate that physical violence according to law is not just allowable, but desirable.

Achieving Control and Effectiveness

Augustine has nothing to say directly about the central problem of civil-military relations: how to achieve a military that is both under the control of the governing structure and effective at war. But drawing inferences from what he does say, we can outline what his theory of control might have looked like.

The most important premise here, as above, is that Augustine has no normative or prescriptive ideas about political order. It is order itself that is important, not the nature of the order. If an individual in a position of civil authority asked Augustine what he ought to do in a specific situation, as his friend Marcellinus did, then Augustine would be happy to advise on Godly conduct. But if one were to ask Augustine to describe the Good City, he would describe the City of God—a realm wholly without politics. Indeed, while Augustine sees humans as naturally social, he does not view politics as a key part of their nature (unlike Plato).

Thus, he also does not have a particular theory of how a government—however constituted—ought to control its military or make it effective. On the one hand, he had significant experience and historical knowledge of military dictatorships in Rome (and other polities), under which the control aspect had mostly to do with preventing specific rival officers from rebelling. On the other hand, he had also seen administrations that were civil in character, which presumably either kept the military under control by paying them sufficiently and governing well (i.e., in a way that did not upset the military) or did not keep control of the military at all. As far as Augustine was concerned, the good soldier would always obey, and anyone who did not obey should be punished if possible. If they rebelled and won, however, they were now in charge and the playing board was reset.

To a certain extent, Augustine may also have believed that a military made up primarily of citizens (i.e., those recognized as being inside the commonwealth and enjoying its benefits) would be more under control than one with large numbers of auxiliaries from conquered peoples, but I have not found any explicit words to that effect.

As for military effectiveness, again, Augustine's focus on the individual soul and on the role of the divine plan indicates that he spent no time considering what human actions might make a military more or less victorious. Wars last as long as God deems them and end when He wants them to, and the victory is bestowed by God, according to his own mysterious plans.

The Soldier's Role in Politics

Finally, can Augustine help us think through the appropriate role of the soldier in politics? This can mean one of four different things: first, the soldier as politician, taking active part in the struggle for power in the polity and the making of laws; second, the soldier as advisor, taking active part in the designing of policy (both foreign and domestic); third, the soldier as domestic enforcer of the laws, forcibly imposing the political order on a possibly resistant public; and fourth, the soldier as citizen, participating in the work of the commonwealth.

Soldier as Politician

As we have seen, order is the prime political good, and thus any extra-institutional struggle against the existing order is a crime against the natural law, which subjects the lower to the higher, and most likely the human law, as well. However, Augustine also believes that some sins are worse than others, and that the intent and role of human passion matter more than the nature of the act, so that it is possible that a crime against order, if done out of a (probably mistaken and prideful) belief that a different order would be more just, is less of a sin than if the rebellion were undertaken out of a lust for power. So much for coup or rebellion.

But what about taking part in the lawful and institutionalized struggle for political power? What if the soldier lives in a democratic republic and wishes to place a finger on the scales of who is in power? Or to be in power themselves? For Augustine, whether this is problematic or not would depend entirely on whether the laws of that polity allowed it or not, and whether the military member undertook the political activity with the right motivation. It seems unlikely that Augustine would think that there is anything in principle that unsuits a member of the military or one with military experience from engaging in the struggle for political power.

Soldier as Advisor

Because of this lack of principled objection to soldiers engaging in political power struggle, it is complicated to infer whether Augustine would have any concept of undue military influence over policy. Certainly, if there are laws in a given polity that specify the parameters of appropriate military advice, then that would define whether influence was undue or not. But would Augustine recognize anything like what Peter Feaver (2003) calls the "relational imperative": The idea that military officers in advisory roles have an obligation not only to give honest, competent advice but also to manage the relationship in such a way that the policymaker's present and future authority and freedom of action are preserved? Let us consider.

From Augustine's perspective, the obligation of the officer is to be a good, Godly person first, and second, to obey the laws and authorities over him. When asked for advice, he should certainly give it honestly and competently, and with respect for the authority asking for the advice. If the officer gives the advice in the hopes of subverting that authority, he is acting with an ill will and therefore sinfully, but if he has no such intention and the authority is nonetheless subverted, Augustine would not call that the fault of the officer.

Both this and the above analysis of soldier as politician indicate a strong correlation between Augustine's perspective and that of those modern military members who, as Risa Brooks (2020: 17–19) describes it, think of themselves as not being political, and therefore expect that any political effect their words or actions may have is simply epiphenomenal; they bear no responsibility for it. It also indicates significant similarity between Augustine and Huntington's general precept that hierarchy and obedience to authority are part of the professional conscience and should take precedence over the individual's conscience (Huntington 1957: 73–9). Augustine's logic makes it very clear that if an officer gives their advice and the political authority does not accept it, the officer should then salute and obey—precisely the result that Huntington says is desirable. In Huntington's logic, this is because the policymaker is the one who has the legitimacy to make policy decisions, whereas the officer has no such legitimacy; in Augustine's logic, it is because the policymaker is in the position of authority. In both cases, the policymaker may be making objectively bad decisions and may be undertaking actions with an ill will or lack of legitimate cause, but this does not matter for the military officer, because he is subject to authority. There is also no room for resistance on the basis of conscience, in Augustine, unless we name as conscience a belief that an order is contrary to God's law. But as we saw above, Augustine is not clear on why some of God's laws can be broken if ordered by authority, but others cannot. In Huntington, it is implicit that, if a soldier cannot reconcile an order with his conscience, he must choose to violate either his professional or his human obligations, and that is a dilemma (Huntington 1957: 120–1).

Soldier as Enforcer

What if the soldier or officer was ordered to enforce the law against fellow citizens? What if the citizens are unhappy with the political order and believe it is wicked or unjust, and are demonstrating against it? What if the soldiery are ordered to repress the demonstration? Huntington insists that militaries should not have any internal role, precisely to prevent them from being confronted with this situation and to prevent them from focusing their training and doctrine on anything but external enemies. But in Augustine's context, it was perfectly normal for soldiers to engage in policing, and it seems clear that his logic of authority would not alter simply because the objects of the violence were fellow citizens rather than foreigners.

If order is the highest earthly good, and soldiers must always obey authority regardless of the justice of the orders, then we can hardly expect them to sympathize with a populace that is unhappy with the order under which they find themselves. Augustine is clear that the breaking of rules and laws ought to be punished, and will be punished, regardless of the justice of the rules, because order must be maintained.

But what if the political order specifically allows for people to demonstrate for their preferred political systems and goals? What if the political order is based on a concept that "the people" should, in some sense, get what they want? This puts the soldier as enforcer in a much more difficult position. Now someone has to assess whether the popular activity falls within the rules, or threatens the political order itself. And if there are some people engaging in clearly legal activity, but others engaging in questionable or illegal activity, at what point does the civil authority decide to treat everyone as a possible malefactor? These are judgment calls where it is possible for people, including people in authority, to disagree over whether a policy or set of orders is consistent with the law or not. Again, Augustine does not really help us understand what to do in the situation of unlawful orders.

Soldier as Citizen

Finally, what about the soldier in his other persona as a citizen or resident of the polity? If the governmental structure is nondemocratic, then few problems arise. But if it is in any sense democratic, then a dilemma arises: how can one simply obey authority if one is responsible for constituting the authority? This is where the political passivity of Augustine's Christianity becomes problematic. Should the Christian support the enactment of laws based on Christian theology, or laws based on the logic of an earthly commonwealth? If Christians are in the minority, should they accept that their views will not be enacted, or should they attempt to convince/convert others to their views? Should the Christian participate in participatory democracy at all? Or simply wait to see what laws are enacted by those who care about such earthly matters and then humbly obey them?

The soldier is in a similar circumstance: should the soldier agitate for certain people, parties, or policies? On the one hand, why not? He is directly affected by the outcomes of the political process and has the right to participate. On the other hand, is it really credible that someone who has overtly agitated for one position and set of policies will simply salute and obey when his political enemies are in authority over him? Would it not be better for the soldier simply to stay out of politics altogether and avoid choosing a party? Does the soldier willingly give up his right to participate in the work of self-governance when he swears to obey whatever government is in place?

While Augustine sometimes talks about republican forms of government and the concept of a commonwealth, he never addresses these questions directly. In fairness, Augustine does not think any true commonwealth can exist in an earthly society, because no earthly society can be truly just. This does not mean that no one should seek to rule justly or seek just laws—Augustine is clear throughout his writings that some bad things are worse than others, and just because perfect justice is not attainable does not mean one should give up on any kind of justice—but it does mean that he simply does not think these kinds of questions are very important. The good Christian is probably not spending a lot of time and effort thinking about the political order of society, because it does not matter that much. Thus there is no point in making the struggle for justice, peace, or a better society one's main pursuit in life; one does one's job and lives under the given rules until one can enjoy true peace and justice in the City of God (cf. Langan 1984: 30–1).

It is worth noting here that although this may seem like a fatalistic attitude, Augustine insists on the freedom of the will (*De libero arbitrio*), and this is another reason that he does not seem to care much about political order: the human will is free and is not subject to structural constraint. Structural constraint, of course, is the idea that one's choices are limited or constrained by one's position in society—one's class, race, gender, wealth, and the like. From Augustine's perspective, every human always has a choice between doing the Godly thing with a Godly will or doing something else. Social constraints are no defense against the demands of righteousness. Individuals have free will, to choose how they will behave in certain situations, but their actions matter only for their eternal fate, they do not change the course of human history away from God's plan.

Conclusion

In some ways, Augustine's thinking pre-figures the conservatism of Huntington, who was influenced mainly by Burke, though I cannot find that either of those gentlemen was directly influenced by reading Augustine. But the pessimism about the earthly existence, including a belief in the inevitability of conflict and thus the necessary evil of war, and a belief that order is in most senses a more important political value than justice (and that order without justice is possible) are common to all three. Burke and Huntington, however, were both explicitly concerned with normative theory about political order, and Augustine is explicitly not. This largely explains the main differences between Augustine and Huntington in terms of the latter's focus on the role of the soldier in politics and the former's near silence on the issue.

In Augustine's view, if one is in the military, especially as an officer, one's first duty is not to do anything that God forbids, and one's second duty is to obey the orders of the constituted authority, regardless of whether those orders seem awful or not. The soldier or officer is not in a position to judge the rightness or wrongness of the war or the things they are ordered to do. Authority is from God, and is given to both good and evil people by God, and the job of those under that authority is not to defy it (unless it asks them to deny God) but to obey it as coming from God. Augustine makes it very clear that he does not consider killing under the color of law to be murder—either in war or in execution—though he does speak of killing the unarmed/innocent as cruel or evil, but attributes that evil to the leader, not the individual soldiers. In terms of the modern questions of civil-military relations, about maintaining political control over the military and the role of the military person in politics, Augustine says very little. We can infer some, but not much that is helpful.

For the most part, Huntington and Augustine would agree; the areas where they would disagree are largely areas that Augustine would simply consider unimportant to the salvation of the soul and thus uninteresting to him. Neither helps us to answer the most pressing questions of civil-military relations in democratic societies, to which we turn in the next chapter.

3

Liberty, Commonweal, Legitimacy, Plurality: Democracy's Highest Political Values

Most of the questions that animate scholars of civil-military relations have to do with issues of government (and military) legitimacy, authority, and effectiveness or competency. In the previous chapter, we saw that, for Augustine, authority and legitimacy are essentially coterminous: if one is in authority, one's orders are legitimate, regardless of whether they conform to some abstract standard of justice, humanity, or competency. But that was in a context of belief in a natural hierarchy not only of soul and body but of some humans over others. The Platonic concept of hierarchical order among humans, which Augustine seems to have adopted, is counter to the modern liberal idea that humans are essentially all equal. The notion that all authority comes from God and is therefore to be obeyed runs counter to the liberal (Lockean/Kantian) idea that humans are individually sovereign and must be treated as ends in themselves. The notion that only the salvation of the soul matters and that no one ought to expend effort on seeking justice or peace on earth runs counter to liberal notions of secularity and justice.

In short, Augustine's views run along very different lines than those of contemporary liberal and/or democratic theorists. For scholars who are interested in governance and civil-military relations in democracies, then, we must determine how democratic theory answers our central questions differently than Augustine (and, to a certain extent, Huntington) did. This chapter will not engage in a comprehensive review of democratic theories but will attempt to examine those aspects of dominant models of democratic thinking that are relevant for our questions here. Those central questions are as follows: what the prime political value is; how the society or polity legitimizes violence, both internally and externally; how the society achieves control over its military while simultaneously ensuring military effectiveness; and what norms or principles govern the soldier's various roles in politics—as politician, advisor, enforcer, and citizen.

Democracy: The Highest Political Value

I have spoken thus far of "democracy" as though everyone knew what that was and agreed that it was good. But "democracy" is a deeply contested term, and we will need to recognize more than one paradigmatic model of it. Schumpeter noted: "We might then define democracy as Rule by the People. Why is that not sufficiently precise? ... because it covers as many meanings as there are combinations between all the possible definitions of the concept 'people' (demos, the Roman populus) and all the possible definitions of the concept 'to rule' (kratein)" (2008: 243). In the 1950s, Robert Dahl called democratic theory "rather unsatisfactory" and noted that there is in fact "no democratic theory, only democratic theories" (Dahl 1956: 1).

Juergen Habermas (1996) argues that there are two classical models of democratic theory (liberal and republican), and he proposes a third (proceduralist-deliberative).[1] I will focus on those three, here, but will note also that critical theorists such as Seyla Benhabib, Iris Marion Young, Sheldon Wolin, and Bonnie Honig (inter alia) have argued that even deliberative democracy does not go far enough in terms of protecting/accepting individual difference

---

[1] Habermas (1996: 23) claims that the original meaning of democracy had to do with "institutionaliz[ing] ... a public use of reason jointly exercised by autonomous citizens," as contrasted with the liberal view of democracy as a market competition among people with given preferences and interests.

(see these authors' contributions in Benhabib 1996a). They argue for more radical forms of democracy in which the prime political value would be pluralism itself. While I take many of their critiques seriously, most of this theorizing is located firmly in the realm of the normative abstract and does not characterize even remotely any actual democratic societies (that I am aware of). Thus, I may refer to these critical theories occasionally but will not treat them fully here.[2]

Liberal (Lockean) Democracy

It is not unusual to hear political rhetoric about "liberal democracy" and "liberal values." But not only are both those terms contested, they are in tension with one another. This creates some irreducible paradoxes and dilemmas for liberal democracy that Augustine did not encounter.

Liberalism generally refers to a set of beliefs that include a view of human beings as equal in their essence (though not in their physical or other endowments), as having an innate right to freedom or liberty in some sense (this is another contested term), and as having an innate right to be treated as ends in themselves, not as means to others' ends (Kant [1797] 2017). Thus, liberalism is inherently a set of beliefs about humans as individuals.

Democracy, on the other hand, is descriptive of some form of sociopolitical organization in which "the people" (however defined) "govern/rule" (however defined) themselves. It is inherently social and about relationships among humans who live in groups. Modern and contemporary theorists of democracy disagree on whether democracy is primarily a method (proceduralists like Schumpeter), a set of specific values (like Arendt), or something more relational (e.g., deliberative or communicative democracy à la Habermas, Benhabib, or Young).

---

[2]To be fair, I am not aware of any actual society that approximates the ideal of deliberative democracy, either, but some might argue that Swiss direct democracy is closer to deliberative ideals than to republican or liberal ones. Ryfe (2005) discusses the literature on deliberative initiatives within polities, but also notes the tendency of deliberative theorists to avoid empirical questions of implementation or functioning.

It is therefore possible to have liberal democracy—which is when the form of organization, communication, and decision-making enshrines or elevates liberal values regarding the individual's rights vis-à-vis both the state and the other members of society—but it is possible to have non-liberal and illiberal forms, as well. As Schumpeter notes, "the relation between democracy and liberty must be considerably more complex than we are in the habit of believing" (2008: 245).

While essential equality is a value of both liberalism and democracy (Kant [1797] 2017), democratic theory has no specific way to answer the question of precisely who is included in that equality or in the form of organization that embodies the equality. Most democratic theory assumes that the group is already defined in some way (cf. Dahl 1956: 53).[3]

One of the biggest tensions between liberalism and democracy is the simple fact of aggregation. What is the most appropriate way to determine what policy ought to be? What the rules ought to be? Each individual may have some ideas, but those must be aggregated in some way. Liberal views of democracy tend to assume that individuals not only are the best judges of what is best for themselves, but that they all know already what their preferences are over any given policy question. If this is the case, aggregation is a simple matter of addition (though that still does not tell us what decision rule ought to hold—whether majority, super-majority, qualified majority, or something else (Dahl 1989, esp. Ch. 10)).

Thus, in liberal democracies, politics is generally seen as a competition among factions. Every person knows their own preferences over every policy question, and creating policy is a matter of competing to win the most votes to one's own party, so that they can make the policies preferred by the majority. Habermas expresses this as "politics has the function of bundling together and pushing private interests against a government apparatus specializing in the administrative employment of political power for collective goals," where society is "a market-structured network of interactions among private persons" (Habermas 1996: 21). This also implies a bright line distinction between the public and private spheres, and that the public sphere should be as limited as possible

---

[3]Though Rousseau recognizes the problem, his account of how a people becomes a people is highly idealized—see *The Social Contract* I.5–6: pp. 361–2.

so as not to interfere in the private actions and interactions of individuals except where absolutely necessary. The role and purpose of government, in Locke's sense, is simply to safeguard the rights every person inherently has to enjoy his/her own life and property with as little interference from others as possible. Again, we may use Habermas's formulation: "The liberal model hinges not on the democratic self-determination of deliberating citizens but on the legal institutionalization of an economic society that is supposed to guarantee an essentially non-political common good by the satisfaction of private preferences" (1996: 27).

In short, the *primary political value* of liberal democracy is the individual liberty of the person, defined mostly as not being subject to interference except for the most limited reasons required for peaceful coexistence. While peace and order are valued as the state in which most people can best enjoy their liberty, the liberty itself is more important than peace and order. In Locke's conception, government arises from a voluntary social contract among people to transfer some of their natural rights to full liberty and self-defense to the society, such that by all giving up some small amount of liberty, they may enjoy and employ their property in the way they want to rather than living in a dangerous state of nature.[4] Should the government, which holds these rights of defense in trust, violate that trust, the contract is null and void and the people are free to make another one.[5]

---

[4] In Locke's view, "freedom of men under government is to have a standing rule to live by, common to every one of that society, and made by the legislative power erected in it. A liberty to follow my own will in all things where that rule prescribes not, not to be subject to the inconstant, uncertain, unknown, arbitrary will of another man" (1999: 122). He goes on:

> There, and there only, is political society where every one of the members hath quitted this natural power [to defend himself and to punish wrongdoers], resigned it up into the hands of the community in all cases that exclude him not from appealing for protection to the law established by it. And thus all private judgment of every particular member being excluded, the community comes to be the umpire. (Locke 1999: 136–7)

[5] It should be noted here that purely procedural concepts of democracy (as, e.g., J. S. Mill might have supported) consider the majority decision to be right/legitimate by virtue of it being the preference of the majority. Madisonian theory, on the other hand, considered the threat of tyranny from the majority to be significant, implying that there were at least some objective standards of right and wrong that were not subject to the process of preference aggregation (cf. Dahl 1956: Ch. 1).

This leads us to the *legitimization of violence* under liberal democracy. For Augustine, the state was justified in using violence to punish rule-breaking if the authorities believed that would best serve the ends of order and individual chastisement (for the sake of righteousness). Augustine was somewhat less enthusiastic about self-defense. While he acknowledged that it could be justified by earthly logic, it was not the best reason to engage in violence. Locke believed that, in the state of nature, everyone ought to refrain from harming any other person "in his life, health, liberty or possessions" (1999: 118). He argued that the only exceptions were defense of one's self and goods against aggression (1999: 136), and "to do justice on an offender."[6] As every human had an inherent right to use violence in defense of their own life or property, this right was what each contracting party transferred (in part) to the government. Thus the government is justified in using violence to defend citizens against attempts by other citizens to attack their lives or property. It is also justified in using violence to enforce the rules of society, since those are in place to secure the liberty of the people to the greatest extent possible. Such use of violence must, however, be only so severe "as will suffice to make it an ill bargain to the offender, give him cause to repent, and terrify others from doing the like" (Locke 1999: 120). Note how similar this is to Augustine's concept of just punishment. In terms of relations between polities, Locke argued that (absent some form of international law) different political entities were in a state of nature with one another and not only could resort legitimately to violence in self-defense, but certainly would (Locke 1999: 137). He does not say this explicitly, but it seems that if political entities are in a state of nature with one another, it would also be legitimate to use violence to acquire things the polity believes it needs for the flourishing of its society.

---

[6]He went on:

> For men being all the workmanship of one omnipotent and infinitely wise maker ... they are His property, whose workmanship they are made to last during His, not another's pleasure. And ... there cannot be supposed any such subordination among us that may authorise us to destroy one another, as if we were made for one another's uses ... Every one ... ought ... to preserve the rest of mankind, and not unless it be to do justice on an offender, take away or impair the life, or what tends to the preservation of the life, the liberty, health, limb, or goods of another. (Locke 118)

Locke never specifically discussed the problem of how to *maintain governmental control* over the military or how to ensure that the society's military was effective. But we can infer from some of his other beliefs that he would have considered any kind of voluntary military service to be a contract which the soldier or sailor was morally obligated to fulfill. The only circumstances under which a member of the military might breach his/her contract would be if the government breached their side of it, or if the entire societal social contract was breached. That may sound like a clear criterion, but of course the issue would be determining exactly what the government's side of the military contract consists of, how to tell when it has been breached, and/or determining exactly when the social contract has broken down to the point that it is no longer binding.

Locke also never discussed specifically what the proper role of the soldier was in society, but again, we can infer.

Soldier as Politician. If politics is a competition among groups for political power in order to enact that group's desired policies, which other groups may not like but must accept as legitimate, then it seems clear that the military as an organization, as part of the government and thus presumably an instrument of the party in power (or possibly opposed to the party in power), should not be allowed to interfere in electoral politics in terms of weighting the competition. If an individual wants to run for political office, they should be free to do that (see "Soldier as Citizen"), but they should have to dissociate themselves from the military organization.

Soldier as Advisor. For the same reasons as above, the military as an organization and individuals acting for the organization or in their corporate capacity should not be able to warp or shape the policymaking process. It is important to recognize that in the liberal conception of democracy, the government's role is limited to making and enforcing the rules necessary for peaceful coexistence; policy should do as little as possible, thus interfering with individual liberty as little as possible. Moreover, policy should reflect the will of the majority of equal individuals, not the will of a group of powerful individuals. Finally, the role of the expert in a liberal conception of democracy is limited to none. While liberals such as Locke believed that every individual knew his ("his" was all that mattered) preferences via his rationality and thus the vote of the majority would in fact produce policy that the majority liked, others such as J. S. Mill ([1859] 1978) acknowledged that sometimes people did not know (or care) what was objectively best for them, but the principle of liberty demanded that they get what they want unless it harmed someone else. Neither of these concepts involves a role for the expert in policymaking—someone who knows how to make "good" policy either by knowing what the actual cause and effect relationships are or by knowing what is actually "best" for the population. Thus there is no justification for an individual or a small group of people—such as military officers—to shape policy according to their ideas and preferences rather than those of the majority.

Soldier as Enforcer. Liberal theorists generally acknowledge the need for the society and the government in particular to use coercive force to maintain individual compliance with the rules. If this is not done, the society falls apart and plunges everyone back into a state of nature, thus destroying the larger liberty they have enjoyed in the social setting. Thus the need for someone to do enforcement is clear. As with Augustine, there is no theoretical reason that the group doing the enforcement should have to be distinct from the military. In Locke's day, there would have been no distinct institution of public and professionalized police. As societies become more complex and specialized, it would make sense to have a separate institution for the separate role of internal enforcement.

Soldier as Citizen. The flip side of the "soldier as politician" logic is that, while the military as an organization cannot interfere in competitive politics, the individual who serves in the military has every right to exercise his or her participatory rights. Military personnel should not be restricted in their individual rights in any way; they should be equal to other citizens. In theory, if they can be trusted to be citizens, they can also be trusted to keep their corporate and individual personae separate.

Republican (Rousseauvian) Democracy

The main early critiques of liberal democracy come in two major forms: first, that it is far too individualistic, which may impair the good of the group as a whole, and second, that majority rule can become a form of tyranny. Rousseau is generally regarded as one of the founding proponents of a different concept of democracy, which came to be thought of as "republican" and can also be thought of as neo-Platonist. In this vision, a people come together to achieve greater liberty and security of person than they can in a state of nature, as with both Hobbes and Locke, but in this society, the sovereign is the General Will, which is defined essentially as what all the people would agree is best for the common good if they were able to discern the common good accurately. Rousseau does not describe it this way—it is a weakness in his theory that he claims both that the General Will arises necessarily from the agreement of all the prospective members of a society and that individuals may not actually be capable of discerning the common good. But his focus on the locus of sovereignty as being in an abstract notion of what all people would agree is best for the collective is quite distinct from the liberal notion that sovereignty remains in the individual, and the realm of politics is simply one of aggregation of preferences. Rousseau sums this up nicely:

> There is often a great difference between the will of all [what all individuals want] and the general will; the general will studies only the common interest while the will of all studies private interest, and is indeed no more than the sum of individual desires. But if we take away from these same wills, the pluses and minuses which cancel each other out, the sum of the difference is the general will. (1999: 366 (II.3))

Habermas states it thus:

> "Politics" is conceived as the reflective form of substantial ethical life, namely as the medium in which the members of somehow solitary communities become aware of their dependence on one another and, acting with full deliberation as citizens, further shape and develop existing relations of reciprocal recognition into an association of free and equal consociates under law ... An autonomous basis in civil society, a basis independent of public administration and market-mediated private commerce is assumed as a precondition for the praxis of civic self-determination. (1996: 21–2)

Rousseau also valued the liberty of the person highly, but his concept of liberty differed from that of Locke (and the later J. S. Mill), in that it involved not simply the "negative freedom from outside interference in one's life, but also a form of "positive" freedom: the freedom to grow as a human beyond the state of nature (governed by instinct) and into a being governed by reason (Rousseau [1762] 1999). Rousseau's basic assumption is that ignorance is bliss; that "natural" man lives in a state of indifference with other humans—neither cooperation nor competition—because his needs are few and easy to satisfy, and he does not know what he does not have. As his experience grows, so do his desires, whereupon he must enter into community with others to satisfy them. This initial entry into community grows organically and leads to the "first inequality"—that of property ownership (Rousseau [1755] 1999). Because those without property are unhappy with this inequality, those with property create political and social institutions to maintain the status quo. This is despotism. Rousseau sought to describe a political organization which would give to humans (really only men) a different kind of liberty than what they had in their solitary ignorance.

In *The Social Contract*, Rousseau looks for "a form of association which defends and protects the person and property of each member with the whole force of the community, and where each, while joining with all the rest, still obeys no one but himself" (I.6: p. 361). Rousseau imagines a society in which all want to be free, all recognize the need to live together to maximize liberty and security of person and property, and all come to a consensus on how this is to be done.[7] This is the General Will, and it is aimed at the common good. Thus, while all are subject to the General Will, because it is general, it is also one's own will, and thus liberty. Habermas (1996: 22) describes it as

> political rights ... of political participation and communication ... guarantee not freedom from external compulsion but the possibility of participation in a common praxis, through the exercise of which citizens can first make themselves into what they want to be—politically autonomous authors of a community

---

[7]"The strongest man is never strong enough to be master all the time, unless he transforms force into right and obedience into duty ... Since no man has any natural authority over his fellows and since force alone bestows no right, all legitimate authority among men must be based on covenants" (Rousseau I.3–4: pp. 358–9).

of free and equal persons ... So, the state's raison d'être lies not primarily in the protection of equal private rights, but in the guarantee of an inclusive opinion- and will-formation in which free and equal citizens reach an understanding on which goals and norms lie in the equal interest of all. (1996: 22)

Rousseau understands that people will not always agree on what the General Will is, but he argues that in the right social environment—one that educates and encourages people to be virtuous themselves and think in terms of the common good rather than their own selfish ends—the majority is more likely to be correct about the General Will than the minority, so the majority should rule in cases where there is not consensus. Thus, as with liberalism, we get an emphasis on majority rule, but for a different reason: under liberalism, the majority is right because they are the majority; under a republican concept, there is a right answer, and the majority are simply more likely to have lit on it than the minority.

Rousseau does not, however, think that sovereignty transfers *away* from the people, as Hobbes does; nor does he allow that the sovereign can ever be located in a single person, except insofar as a delegation of power, because that individual will always have particular interests in conflict with the General Will. He says, "If a people promises simply and solely to obey, it dissolves itself by that pledge; it ceases to be a people; for once there is a master, there is no longer a sovereign, and the body politic is therefore annihilated" (II.1: p. 365).[8]

All thinkers in the republican tradition share a concern with the ability (or lack thereof) of the majoritarian principle to yield a well-governed state and believe that, for true liberty to exist, the laws must be made by the wise and virtuous and with the object of the common good. So we may say that the *primary political value* in republican democracy is also the liberty of the individual but conceived differently from that of the liberals. Liberty in the republican tradition requires not merely non-interference but freedom from any exercise of arbitrary power; in short, it requires active self-governance and active participation in the life of the society. This in turn requires people to be both virtuous and

---

[8] He goes on to note that "the commands of leaders may ... pass for the general will if the sovereign, being free to oppose them, does not do so" (II.1: p. 365).

well-informed. A republican conception of democracy leaves almost no room for a private sphere; nearly everything is part of the life of the society, and one's individual virtue and personal development are of direct interest to the polity as a whole. Furthermore, Rousseau is clear that there are values that rank higher than mere order:

> It will be said that a despot gives his subjects the assurance of civil tranquillity. Very well, but what does it profit them, if those wars against other powers which result from a despot's ambition, if his insatiable greed, and the oppressive demands of his administration cause more desolation than civil strife would cause? What do the people gain if their very condition of civil tranquillity is one of their hardships? There is peace in dungeons, but is that enough to make dungeons desirable? (I.4: p. 359)

As for the *legitimization of violence*, most republican thinkers agree that the state has the right and the duty to use coercive force to punish those who violate the social contract and in general to maintain the common good, including defense from outside threats. However, it is important to note that Rousseau thinks a society that features a significant amount of deviation and need for punishment is a failing society; if people are properly educated and habituated, they will understand and agree with the General Will and not deviate from it. For Rousseau, the way to get a people to recognize and follow the General Will is, first, for the people (those participating, anyway—Rousseau is not a universalist and would exclude women from public life) to be "properly informed." This means both properly educated and having consistent access to accurate information. Second, to prevent any factions or "sectional associations" from forming in the society in the first place (because that will overwhelm the General Will with the will of a particularly powerful group), or, failing that, to multiply them so as to prevent one from dominating (II.3; also cf. Madison [1787] 1961: 45–52 (Federalist Paper no. 10)).

For Rousseau, unlike Locke, there is no higher law than that of the sovereign exercising the General Will:

> A public decision can impose an obligation on all subjects towards the sovereign ... [but] cannot impose an obligation on the sovereign towards itself ... it would be against the very

nature of a political body for the sovereign to set over itself a law which it could not infringe ... there neither is, nor can be, any kind of fundamental law binding on the people as a body, not even the social contract itself. (I.7: pp. 362–3)

Within the contract, however, the sovereign is justified in using coercion to prevent individual members from disobeying the General Will—that is, the laws (I.7: pp. 362–3; II.4: pp. 367–8).[9] The sovereign is also justified in using force against other groups or sovereigns in the defense of its own group.

Unlike Augustine, Rousseau's view of war is fairly limited:

War, then, is not a relation between men, but between states; in war individuals are enemies wholly by chance, not as men, not even as citizens, but only as soldiers; not as members of their country, but only as its defenders ... The foreigner—whether he is a king, a private person or a whole people—who robs, kills, or detains the subjects of another prince without first declaring war against that prince, is not an enemy but a brigand. Even in the midst of war, a just prince, seizing what he can of public property in the enemy's territory, nevertheless respects the persons and possessions of private individuals; he respects the principles on which his own rights are based. Since the aim of war is to subdue a hostile state, a combatant has the right to kill the defenders of that state while they are armed; but as soon as they lay down their arms and surrender, they cease to be either enemies or instruments of the enemy; they become simply men once more, and no one has any longer the right to take their lives. It is sometimes possible to destroy a state without killing a single one of its members, and war gives no right to inflict any more destruction than is necessary for victory. (I.4: pp. 359–60)

---

[9] [The state] must have a universal and compelling power to move and dispose of each part in whatever manner is beneficial to the whole ... the social pact gives the body politic an absolute power over all its members; and it is this same power which, directed by the general will, bears, as I have said, the name of sovereignty. (II.4)

Later, he says of the covenant among the people, "It is a legitimate covenant, because its basis is the social contract; an equitable one, because it is common to all; a useful one, because it can have no end but the common good; and it is a *durable covenant because it is guaranteed by the armed forces* and the supreme power" (II.4; emphasis added).

Like most other early theorists of democratic governance, Rousseau does not specify a theory of how to *maintain government or civil control* over the military, or how to make the military an effective instrument of power. In general, these things are simply assumed. We can infer, though, that he thinks members of society should be willing to serve in the military when necessary for the defense of society and that they should be obedient for reasons of conscience and principle. He says,

> [The people's] very lives, which they have pledged to the state, are always protected by it; and even when they risk their lives to defend the state, what more are they doing but giving back what they have received from the state? What are they doing that they would not do more often, and at greater peril, in the state of nature ... Assuredly, all must now fight in case of need for their country, but at least no one has any longer to fight for himself ... when the prince says to him: "It is expedient for the state that you should die," then he should die, because it is only on such terms that he has lived in security as long as he has. (II.4–5: pp. 368–9)

What does a republican form of democracy indicate about the various roles a soldier can occupy in society?

Soldier as Politician. It is important to note that republican concepts of representation differ significantly from one thinker to the next. Rousseau did not think that the sovereignty of the people could be delegated to representatives (it had to remain a collective but abstract entity) but that the administration of laws could be. To the extent that he believed in representative government, he envisioned a sort of elective aristocracy: the administration should be made up of men elected by the people on the basis of their virtue and wisdom. Madison's compromise between liberal and republican forms of democracy was manifested partly in anti-majoritarian institutions designed to constrain the House of Representatives and involve a measure of aristocratic principle.

Given that both Madison and Rousseau would have equated military officers with the upper classes, it seems likely that early republican thinking would have had no issue with an officer wishing to be involved in electoral or representative office, assuming that officer were a man of virtue, wisdom, and merit. Given the general view of regular soldiers (as opposed to officers) as lazy and vicious, a republican concept would probably exclude them from any role in government, but not as soldiers per se.

So much for holding office. But what about involvement in electoral politics in other ways? Here we get into the difficult question of representation, and it is difficult to claim that there would be one republican position on the issue. Given the republican emphasis on the need for men of virtue, wisdom, and expertise to bear the lion's share of the work of governing, we may assume that they would not exclude military personnel as such. On the other hand, the republican fear of faction or sectional interests overwhelming the General Will seems to indicate that they would be concerned about an institutionalized military holding too much political power, and thus perhaps would prefer a noninstitutionalized military. This would imply a preference for a militia model or possibly a foreign legion model, in which no member of the society would ever encounter a tension between his identity as a citizen and his identity as a soldier. If the society were to determine that, for security reasons, they required a standing army of professionals, we might expect them to attempt to weaken the institution vis-à-vis the civilian administration.

Soldier as Advisor. Unlike in the liberal conception, the republican ideal of democracy has a role for the expert. Policy aims at the common good, or at the right thing, and this means that the advice of the wise and virtuous is desirable. To the extent that military officers (again, likely only officers) can help the administration make policy in the best interests of the common good, therefore, their role is appropriate. If, however, they are acting in their own corporate interest rather than that of the whole society, that is inappropriate and undesirable.

It seems unlikely that republican theory would yield any specific guidance as to whose preferences should prevail in case of disagreement, as the idea is that these wise, virtuous, rational people should naturally converge on the best concept, if they deliberate sufficiently. But in extremis, republican theory would probably favor the expert over the elected official, as more likely to be discerning the proper General Will.

Soldier as Enforcer. As with liberal democracy, republican democracy allows for the use of coercive force to maintain the rule of law. As with liberal democracy, there does not seem to be any reason of principle why the military could not fulfill this role.

Soldier as Citizen. In republican views of democracy, it is absolutely essential that citizens participate actively in the life of the society. Unlike liberal democracy, where society exists largely to allow the individual to pursue their individual desires without interference, in republican democracy, society is the complex in which the individual is fully actualized. Thus, while republican theories would not expect enlisted persons and lower-ranking officers to play a large role in the actual legislation or administration, it would insist on their being allowed and encouraged to vote, to debate, and to participate in the political life of the society.

Deliberative Democracy

As noted above, liberal democracy assumes that people know their preferences and they simply need to be aggregated or counted up, then executed through a state apparatus (see Habermas 1996; Young 1996). Republican democracy indicates that there is a preference that all members of society agree on, or would agree on if they were properly educated, informed, and habituated. But what if pluralism is irreducible? And what if people do not already know all their preferences? And what if people's preferences could change based on gaining a greater understanding of their neighbors' beliefs, experiences, and the like?

Deliberative democracy holds that what makes a system democratic is whether it allows/encourages/engages all citizens equally in conversation about collective issues such that they understand the issues better, grow to understand (and potentially change) their own preferences, and engage in rule/decision-making together (see Benhabib 1996b; Cohen 1996; Young 1996). This is in some ways similar to the republican ideal of the common good/General Will, but deliberative democracy does not assume that the common good is objective and simply needs to be discovered; deliberation serves rather to generate and create, not simply reveal.[10] Habermas (1996: 25) notes that "the deliberative mode of legislative practice

---

[10] Note that this is the theory. Empirical research raises significant questions about whether this actually works. As Ryfe notes, "Deliberation represents a disturbance of everyday reasoning habits" (2005: 56) and is both difficult to bring about and not guaranteed to produce positive social or decisional results.

is not intended just to ensure the ethical validity of laws. Rather ... to compromise competing interests in a manner compatible with the common good, and, on the other hand, to bring universalistic principles of justice into the horizon of the specific form of life of a particular community."[11]

Discourse theory "invests the democratic process with normative connotations stronger than those found in the liberal model but weaker than those of the republican model ... [it] has the success of deliberative politics depend not on a collectively acting citizenry but on the institutionalization of the corresponding procedures and conditions of communication" (Habermas 1996: 27). Sheldon Wolin calls democracy "a project concerned with the political potentialities of ordinary citizens, that is, with their possibilities for becoming political beings through the self-discovery of common concerns and of modes of action for realizing them" (1996: 31).

Identifying the *primary political value* of deliberative models is difficult precisely because deliberative democracy is mainly proceduralist and not focused on the content of outcomes. It is also still a deeply debated and contested concept. We may infer, however, that the primary value for deliberative theorists is that all people are actively included in the process of deliberating about what kind of society they want to constitute and what rules they want to live by.

There is significant disagreement among deliberative theorists about whether *coercion is ever legitimate* or how it is properly legitimized. Jane Mansbridge (1996) argues that some amount of coercion will always be necessary in a democracy in order to avoid over-privileging the status quo.[12] She also notes, however, that in

---

[11]Habermas (1996) argues specifically for a proceduralist form of deliberative democracy that relies on a set of agreed-upon procedures to help legitimize the processes of deliberation and dialogue, but other forms are possible. For Habermas, "according to this proceduralist view, practical reason withdraws from universal human rights, or from the concrete ethical substance of a specific community, into the rules of discourse and forms of argumentation. In the final analysis, the normative content arises from the very structure of communicative actions" (1996: 26).

[12]When individual interests come in what gives every indication of being an irreconcilable conflict, a democratic polity must either reinforce the status quo by taking no action or, by taking action, force or threaten (coerce) some of its citizens into situations or actions not in their interests. Majority rule is one standard mechanism for achieving a relatively fair form of democratic coercion (Mansbridge 1996: 47).

a context of lasting disagreement (i.e., in an irreducibly pluralistic society), no justification for coercion will ever be accepted by every group as fair. Thus legitimization for coercion in such a society will always be just "good enough" rather than complete. She notes that in a complex, interdependent society, there will be countless occasions

> in which collective action requires some degree of coercion to attain even unanimously approved collective ends. And because in a large society with a number of conflicting interests the requirement of unanimity will give almost total power to those who benefit from the status quo, democracies committed to some rough approximation of equal power will require some forms of nonunanimously approved coercion to attain ends that most of their citizens approve. (Mansbridge 1996: 48)

This view stands in contrast to the republican view that the General Will will achieve unanimity, and that a society that requires coercion to maintain the rules is a society that is essentially already failing. It also stands in contrast to the proceduralist view that, while there will never be unanimity on what the substance of policy should be, there can be unanimity on what constitutes legitimate procedure, and such agreement will cause the losers of any particular policy battle to accept the outcome without coercion.

I have yet to encounter a deliberative theorist who addressed the role of the military in society or even how government would function in a practical sense.[13] Thus I cannot articulate their views on achieving both *control and effectiveness*.

---

[13]Wolin, indeed, argues that "democracy needs to be reconceived as something other than a form of government" (1996: 43). He does not even list the military or police power among the "components of state power" (Wolin 1996: 36). This being said, there is a literature on the implementation of deliberation (see Ryfe 2005, for a review), but it is focused more on the issue of how more deliberation can be introduced into existing systems of government and less on how one would embody the normative theory as a whole system. It is of course possible that that is the extent of the idea of deliberation—that it could work within multiple forms of administration—but again, none of this literature addresses the specific questions of military or bureaucratic control.

The Soldier's Role in Politics

Soldier as Politician. Mansbridge notes that "in a good democracy, large or small, the deliberative arena should ideally be equally open to all, and power—in the sense of the threat of sanction or the use of force—should not interfere with the impact of the better argument" (1996: 47).

Soldier as Advisor. Deliberative/discourse theory does not provide any insight on this issue.

Soldier as Enforcer. Again, even the concept of enforcement is not universally agreed upon among deliberative theorists. To the extent that some believe enforcement will be a necessary part of governance, they provide no reason to think that it must be done by an organization separate from the one that defends the state from external threats.

Soldier as Citizen. One of the main concepts theorists of deliberative democracy rely on is that of civil society as a set of relationships and norms that eventually take on enough strength and meaning that they balance out other forms of power in society (such as money or control of administrative apparatus) (see, e.g., Habermas 1996: 28). In this sense, the member of the military not only has as much right to participate in the general processes of deliberation and sense-making, but is also a critical part of the whole, if the ideal of free and equal citizens is to be realized. The soldier or officer therefore should not be restricted from participation in full political rights.

Conclusions

Democratic theorists are divided on how to deal with some of the central dilemmas of the concept of rule by the people: How to determine who "the people" are? How to determine what "the people" want? How to determine when the people should get what they want, and when they should not? And perhaps most importantly: Is democracy legitimated by the fact that it is rule by the people (procedural)? Or is it legitimated by the fact that rule by the people is most likely to produce the best outcomes for the people (civil and political rights, good or at least moderate policy, political stability, pluralism, liberty) (Benhabib 1996b; Cohen 1996: 97)?

Different groups of theorists answer these questions differently. All disagree to some extent with Augustine about the nature of the primary political value: for Augustine it was order; for democratic theorists, it is variously liberty in a negative sense (of freedom from arbitrary interference), liberty in a positive sense (of participation, civic virtue, and collective governance), and/or inclusion. Most agree that some level of coercion by the state is necessary and justified, but all also agree that state coercive violence should be somewhat limited. Both liberal and civic republican theorists agree that a state should defend its residents from outside threat, and to some extent imply that even wars of aggression may be justified for the good of the polity.

Few theorists of democracy have dealt directly with the issue of how to achieve a military that is both effective and obedient; indeed, few mention the military or the state apparatus at all (except Madison). We will see in the following chapter how other scholars have tried to fill in these details; here we can only extrapolate. All forms agree that the individual service-member should not have to give up their rights to civic participation—they should have and exercise the right to vote, to deliberate, to take active part in the political life of society. All also agree, to the extent that they believe enforcement is necessary, that there is no principled reason the military could not carry out that enforcement. Where they do somewhat differ is in the role of the military officer as political advisor, and in the extent to which members of the military ought to be able to run for and hold political office. In terms of advising, the liberal model is less sanguine about this, but not because of the nature of the military so much as because the liberal model elevates the preferences of the people as aggregated through the society's preferred procedure over the idea of a small elite making policy. Civic republican and deliberative theorists might both see a larger role for the idea of expert advice in policymaking. Finally, while their notions of representation differ, and therefore not all theorists would answer the question of military politicians the same way, we can infer that all theorists of democracy would disapprove of the military as an institution (including the military service-member acting in their capacity as a service-member) being involved in electoral politics. They might have different views of the appropriateness of individual service-members running for or being appointed to office, depending on their relative valuing of merit, virtue, and wisdom (and how far they see those embodied in military officers).

Only Madison, of all the theorists we have considered, spent significant time discussing the role of the military, and his attitude was that the institution was a dangerous one and should be kept both small and deeply integrated with society, but he never indicated an opposition to the idea of former officers serving in elected or appointed office. Indeed, given the model of mostly amateur and sporadic officership at the time he was writing, it would have been nearly impossible to keep the political and military elite entirely separate (Madison [1787] 1961: esp. Federalist Papers 10, 18, 19, 20, and 51).[14]

In the next chapter, we shall consider how political scientists, historians, and sociologists have attempted to operationalize some of these ideas, and what they have discovered in their empirical studies of militaries and democratic breakdown.

---

[14]Page ranges for the Federalist Papers are as follows: 10 (pp. 45–52), 18 (pp. 90–6), 19 (pp. 96–102), 20 (pp. 102–6), and 51 (pp. 288–93). Also, Hamilton was a co-author for papers 18–20.

4

Militaries and Democratic Breakdown

If we cannot derive a clear professional ethic from the democratic theories, is it possible to derive one from the empirical record? Are there patterns to how militaries contribute to democratic breakdown, or to how they can slow or even stop it? Are there certain attitudes or behaviors that are better or worse for the survival of democratic governance and institutions? This chapter will explore first what normative civil-military relations thinkers have said about our framing questions, and second, what we know empirically about the roles that militaries have played in governance and regime change, to determine whether we can reach inductively what has so far eluded us deductively.

One dilemma introduced by democratic theory is the tension between a commitment to pure process and a commitment to content. On one end of the spectrum of democratic theory is the idea that democracy consists of process and that process must be respected no matter what laws or rules it produces. This is the majoritarian/libertarian view, and is closer to Augustine's view of the overwhelming importance of order and respect for authority rather than the morality of the laws. On the other end of the spectrum is the idea that democracy is legitimate largely because it is the process most likely to produce and safeguard certain substantive outcomes, like civil liberty, protections for permanent minorities, and the like. This is somewhat more of a civic republican view, though some advocates of deliberative democracy tend to imply that deliberation would also produce better outcomes than the pure process version. The dilemma for the military officer sworn to uphold democratic governance and institutions, however, is that neither of these models exists in its pure form, and therefore they must determine when they are to defend the process and when the outcome. Indeed, as Linz (1978: 53) has put it, one of the sources of the "unsolvable problem" that begins the downward spiral of democratic breakdown is, "who is to argue that political leaders should sacrifice staunchly held policy goals, the interests of their followers, or their image of a good society for the sake of the persistence of political institutions that do not seem to serve the pursuit of those aims?"

The literature on democratic breakdown rarely focuses on the military as an actor (Belkin and Schofer 2003: 596; Kuehn 2017: 788–9), probably because even though coup is the single most common element in the failure of transitioning democracies (Bell 2016; Thyne and Powell 2019), it is still fairly uncommon, and it is almost never the case that the military acts in a political vacuum. In other words, even though military coup may be the proximate cause of the downfall of a transitioning democratic government, it will almost certainly not be attempted until and unless there are other significant elements of public unrest or dissatisfaction. The military does not delegitimize a government; a decline in the legitimacy of the government provides an opportunity for the military to take, if it so chooses.

The chapter proceeds as follows: I first discuss the classic arguments for what elements a military professional ethic should include, particularly in a democratic context, and why such an ethic is so important. Many scholars have identified the political, social, and moral dilemmas in which military personnel may find themselves, in which the law cannot give them satisfactory guidance and they need a code of ethics to help them make decisions. Second, I discuss the empirical literature on military involvement in politics and governance, specifically the literature on coups, military response to mass protests/civil unrest, and other forms of domestic military activity that may weaken democratic norms and institutions. The chapter concludes with some helpful insights, but ultimately finds that it is not possible to specify a list of behaviors that ought to be prohibited under all circumstances. The issue remains that it is not always the behavior itself that is important, but its intended and actual effects on democratic institutions.

Existing Arguments on Professional Ethics

Peter Feaver (1996) described the civil-military problematique as the issue of how to get a military that is both strong and competent enough to defend the state, and subordinate enough not to use its strength and competency against the state. But the dilemma of the democratic military professional ethic is slightly different: how to get military professionals whose allegiance is neither to a specific regime or person nor to a higher concept of the state defined by their own judgment. This is rarely an issue in nondemocratic states, where most coup-proofing techniques focus on creating close identity between the interests of the officer corps and the interests of the ruling regime (party, religion, family, language group, etc.). But in democratic states, where we want the military officer corps to accept both that the person and party in power will change regularly, and that whatever person or party is in power has the legitimacy to determine the direction of the state, but also that the person or party in power might try to undermine the fundamental nature of the system and violate the spirit of the laws, which it is also their duty to defend, it becomes clear why developing a specific ethic is so difficult. Feaver (2003) pointed out that civilian policymakers have the right to be wrong, but they do not have the right to be wrong about everything. They do not, for example, have the right to be wrong about the meaning of election results. But how is the military officer to act when the political official is violating not just the officer's concept of wise policy, but their understanding of democratic process?

Many great scholars have thrown their hats in the ring on this issue, but all have struggled to produce an ethic that would function for all democracies. Fitch (1998), indeed, argues that there is no one-size-fits-all ethic, because its content must depend on the particular political, social, and historical context of the society. But as Stepan (1988: 13) makes clear, nearly all agree that the content of military professionalism matters in some sense.

We have already discussed Huntington's view of the appropriate professional ethic as one that focuses on the defense of the state from external enemies, on the development of "purely military" skill and expertise, on the self-exclusion of the officer from all political questions and issues, predicated on the policymakers granting them full autonomy in their own sphere, and on the concept that they are public servants with responsibility to the society. Janowitz (1960), a sociologist and Huntington's contemporary, argued that the professional officer was not functionally constrained to have a certain ideological bent or worldview, as Huntington argued they were, nor was it effective and useful for them to think of themselves as separate and necessarily different from the society they defended; they should mirror as closely as possibly the values of the society. However, in the end, Janowitz, too, thought that military officers should obey the orders of the policymakers and refrain from involvement in political activity, and agreed with Huntington that the main mechanism for that was a professional ethic of self-restraint (Burk 2002; Cohn 2011).

Sarkesian pushed back on this ideal of a military separated from political activity, arguing that an apolitical professionalism was both unrealistic and dysfunctional. He argued, *contra* Huntington, that the changing natures of both society and war made it practically impossible to distinguish the purely military from the purely political (1981: 285). He thought that "the requisites of a democratic ideology … do not provide for a separate subsystem removed from society. The legitimacy and credibility of any military system rests with its links to society and the reflection of basic social values" (290). He describes this ideal model as equilibrium:

> The model presumes that the military profession is composed of an educated elite whose role in society is the organization, control, and application of force in pursuit of democratic values as determined by the state. Complementing this is the concept that the profession not only controls and supervises the military instrument in accordance with established policy, but that professional morals and ethics require a commitment to democratic ideals which in turn presuppose a role in the political process. In brief, the equilibrium model presumes that the various subsystems share the same values and agree upon the norms of behavior. Moreover, in the case of the military and society, each maintains its own integrity and identity, but political-psychological support to all individuals, regardless of whether they are military or civilian, emanate from the political-social order. This is reinforced by the fact that the military exists

for the sole purpose of supporting the democratic political-social order. To do this properly, the military must be committed to such a system, understand it, and reflect its basic value structure within the military institution. (290–1)

Sarkesian goes on to argue that it is appropriate for military officers and the military institution to participate in the "politics" of pursuing its institutional interests, particularly in the unofficial sphere, so long as their role in the official sphere of politics remains strictly limited (291). He argues that military officers must recognize that their relationship with the civilian world is both symbiotic and asymmetrical—while the military is "committed to defend the state, democratic values, and the existing political system, [it] does not have a major role in determining the norms or boundaries of the political power of political actors" (292). For him, this means that military officers ought to receive a thorough education to help them understand and appreciate the political and social dimensions of both their own society and of conflict; that they should be politically aware, astute, and committed to democracy, but not engage in any activity supporting a political party over another (293). His view of a professional ethic involves enlightened advocacy, which he describes thus:

Advocacy means the articulation of a particular point of view or policy while attempting to influence the political system to accept such a point of view or policy. Enlightened advocacy therefore presumes not only the advocation of a particular position or point of view, but also that this be done with sophistication and maturity within the accepted principles of liberal democratic society. (294)

Stepan, a leading scholar of democracy and militaries in Latin America, argues: "For polities that aspire to be democracies, a complex range of norms, institutions, and practices must be constructed socially, constantly reconstructed, and continually brought to bear so that a democratic polity in fact shapes, monitors, and controls the means of force" (1988: ix–x). Later, he also notes that democracy requires free and fair elections (6), which implies that militaries should not interfere in elections that are already free and fair, but what if political actors are interfering to make the elections unfree and unfair? Here we begin to see the difficulty in simply listing actions the military can/should or cannot/should not do. They should not interfere in good elections; should they interfere in bad ones? If the actors trying to interfere with elections are outside the regime, it is within reason to imagine the regime ordering the military to protect the elections—this was done frequently by the US federal government during Reconstruction, and states use National Guard personnel to conduct cyber-security for elections (Hughes 2022). But what if the actor(s) trying to interfere in the election are in the regime and looking to solidify power? What if their position is legitimate, but their actions are not? Stepan (1988: 111–12) argues that the military qua military should have no deliberative role in a democracy; that they should not have discretion in their obedience to legitimate authority. And this is of course the default normative position. But we all recognize that there are conceivable situations where we would prefer that the military not obey (Robinson, Cohn, and Margulies 2021). The difficulty is in developing an ethic that helps military servicemembers—as well as the rest of us—determine when to bring their personal and/or professional discretion into play.

Fitch (1998) states: "In regimes with institutionalized democratic control, the armed forces voluntarily accept civilian control because they have internalized democratic norms. Military role beliefs stressing political and professional subordination are considered legitimate and binding; antidemocratic role beliefs are marginalized or nonexistent in the officer corps" (41). Fitch goes on to describe a few different types of professionalism (in terms of the officers' role beliefs), one of which he calls "democratic professionalism." In this, he posits an ultimate allegiance to the nation, rather than the state (175), and an acknowledgment that "democratic regimes [are] the only authentic expression of the shared interests and majority preferences of the nation, which the armed forces are sworn to defend" (175). But he also acknowledges that it is precisely this mindset that offers militaries the opportunity to deliberate and use their own discretion that he and others argue cannot be appropriate for militaries in a democracy:

> From the viewpoint of modern political theory, this transformation of military patriotism into a justification for military intervention in politics is untenable. National identities are

complex and constantly evolving ... Given conflicting views of national identity in ideologically pluralistic societies, who then is empowered to define national values and national interests? In democratic societies, the answer is clear: only the duly elected representatives of the nation. The key premise of democratic professionalism is thus the rejection of any military claim to a suprapolitical role as national guardians. Democratic theory denies the claim of any individual or group to represent the "national will" or define "national interests." Only a fully enfranchised electorate can speak for the nation as a whole. (176)

Again, this leaves us with no solution to the problem of what to do when the regime itself appears to be losing its legitimacy in the eyes of "the people," or when it appears to be engaging in deliberate sabotage of the electoral system or the civil and political rights of the people. The military are to internalize "democratic norms," but which ones? They are to obey the will of the people as expressed through legitimate representative institutions, but what if there is disagreement over how legitimate those institutions are?

Dissatisfied with the Huntingtonian arguments stressing separation between the political and the military, Cohen (2001, 2002) developed an idea he called the "unequal dialogue." In this conceptualization, the military and the political are not divided into discrete spheres but engage as human beings in a dialogue meant to be productive and serve the public good. This is not, however, a dialogue of equals, but one in which the military recognizes its subordinate yet crucial position. The policymakers are in a sense dependent upon the military advisors, but that dependency ought to activate in the military officers a professional respect for their own subordinate role and their duty to the public. While this callback to Sarkesian helps the military officer understand that they need not shy away from political discussion, it continues to rely in the last instance on the officer's own acknowledgment that there are certain things they ought not to do, and their own self-restraint in not doing them, even though they can.

How to get at the contents of this professional ethic that is supposed to encourage military officers to develop their expertise, conceive of themselves as critical to society's well-being, and advise potentially far less-experienced policymakers, yet also to restrain them from taking advantage of any of their power to do what they think is best for society? Burk (2002) argues eloquently that there is a distinction between a military that protects democratic values and one that sustains them. The former is there to protect the integrity and sovereignty of the state from external threats and need not embody or even respect liberal and democratic values in order to do its job. The latter must "in crucial respects identify substantively with and so embody the values of the society it defends" (Burk 2002: 12). The former attitude Burk associates with Huntington, the latter with Janowitz (1960). What, specifically, are these values? Burk argues that civilian control of the military is only one of them, and not the most important one. He lists a reliance on reason and persuasion as opposed to coercion, respect for the rights—"civil, political, and social"—and sovereignty of the people, transparency and accountability in public policy, made by political representatives, who are chosen in fair and frequent elections (Burk 2002: 8).

Again, these are excellent values, but some of them are substantive, and some of them are procedural. What happens when the substantive and procedural are in conflict?

In his wide-ranging study of how to build militaries in transitioning democracies, Barany (2012) cites Morgenthau to bolster his claim that democracies should not strive for "a politically neutral military but [for] one that is firmly committed to democratic governance" (2012: 32). He lists a number of important structural factors but emphasizes that "the critical objective of democratizing states is to increase the military's professionalism" (34), by which he means essentially a military that is properly trained and educated in its functional requirements, but also one with an "organizational culture of self-restraint, deference to the constitution, and recognition of the sacrifices society makes for its defense" (34). These seem like values with which no well-intentioned person could argue, until one notices that different groups in society may interpret the law and the constitution in varying ways.

Nearly all of these concepts challenge Huntington in some sense—primarily the sense that militaries should be politically "sterile" or without political or even social identity aside from identifying with the state or the nation. But they also all struggle with a similar set of problems: should the military have discretion, or not? Should it internalize democratic values and prioritize a democratic system, or be politically sterile and neutral? What would it mean to internalize democratic values? What do they do when two apparently democratic values are in tension? They should obey the law, but what happens when the law has lost legitimacy? What happens when the state and the nation are at odds? The next section will attempt to sort out whether there is a solution available from the inductive side.

Empirical Literature

Coups

Nearly all the literature on coups agree that they pose a significant threat to nondemocracies and transitioning or unconsolidated democracies but much less so to mature or consolidated democracies (Thyne and Powell 2019; Powell et al. 2018; Svolik 2015; Bell 2016; Kuehn 2017; Londregan and Poole 1990); that they are the primary mode by which democracies fall (Kieh and Agbese 2005; Thyne and Powell 2019); but that that statistic is driven by their occurrence in unconsolidated or transitioning democracies, and that any given coup is more likely to overthrow an authoritarian leader than a democratically elected one (Thyne and Powell 2019).

There is wide agreement that coup risk is higher in countries with low levels of economic development (Londregan and Poole 1990; Svolik 2015; Thyne and Powell 2019) and a history of coups (Belkin and Schofer 2003; Svolik 2015; Thyne and Powell 2019). There is mixed evidence on whether more democratic/liberal/pluralist societies are more, less, or equally coup-prone (Johnson et al. 1984; Svolik 2015; Bell 2016; Thyne and Powell 2019). There is also mixed evidence on whether militaries with some internal security role are more likely to intervene in politics than those with a purely external orientation (Johnson et al. 1984; Stepan 1988: 13; Fitch 1998: esp. 120–3; Pion-Berlin and Trinkunas 2005; Pion-Berlin, Esparza, and Grisham 2014: esp. 243–5; Brooks 2022: 7; Jenne and Martinez 2022; Cohn 2022).[1] Finally, scholars disagree

---

[1]Some authors argue that having a military do internal security missions—or any internal missions at all—can be detrimental to democratic institutions (Stepan 1986; Stepan 1988; Fitch 1998: esp. 121–3; Desch 2001; Bove, Rivero, and Ruffa 2020; Kyle and Reiter 2021; Jenne and Martínez 2022). This is supposed to happen

on whether the level of "professionalization" matters significantly, and more importantly, they disagree on the direction in which it matters (Stepan 1988; Fitch 1998: esp. 2–3, 7; Kamrava 2000; Albrecht and Ohl 2016: 40).[2]

The single factor that nearly all coup researchers agree on that forms a proximate cause of coup is the military's organizational self-interest and a fear that that interest is threatened (Finer 1962; Nordlinger 1977; Barany 2012; Singh 2014; Bell 2016; Sudduth 2017; Kuehn 2017; Thyne and Powell 2019).

The other main point of agreement is that coups occur when there is a crisis of government legitimacy (Finer 1962; Nordlinger 1977; Stepan 1988; Linz 1990; Fitch 1998; Belkin and Schofer 2003; Marinov and Goemans 2014; Bodea, Elbadawi, and Houle 2017; Bell 2016; Thyne and Powell 2019; Chiozza and Khalifa 2023). Such a crisis may result in major public unrest or demonstrations, which may draw the military into the fray either willingly or unwillingly (see Section "Behavior during Mass Protests"), or it may cause the military to fear for its own interests. We will explore later in the chapter what factors generally cause crises of government legitimacy.

In terms of actions that ought to be taken or not, there is a general agreement that coups against democratic regimes are normatively undesirable; that militaries should not remove the government and replace it with themselves or some other group (Finer 1962; Nordlinger 1977). But this ignores the fact that one of the problems potentially leading up to a coup is precisely the question of whether

---

primarily via a strengthening of the military organization vis-à-vis other government agencies in terms of its budget, its prestige, its level of trust among the population, and (resultantly) its bargaining power. It is also supposed to increase the military's self-conception of having a stake in potentially highly politicized issues, and thus in having a right to deliberate on and have discretion over the appropriate response to such issues. This is all believed to be a danger regardless of whether the military wanted these missions in the first place or accepted them only reluctantly (Stepan 1988: esp. 111–12). However, some authors have noted that such internal mission orientations do not necessarily result in these negative outcomes (Fitch 1998; Cohn 2022) and that these outcomes are most likely conditional on other factors.

[2] In most of this literature, "professionalization" is operationalized as military education, meritocratic promotion criteria, and formalized institutional structures, because these are easier to observe and measure than the existence, extent, and content of norms. The idea of "professionalism" will be explored further in the next chapter.

the regime is, in fact, democratic, or democratically legitimate. Now we would appear to be faced with the question of whether it is more important for a military never to remove a government, or for a government to be democratically legitimate. This may in turn be a misleading framing of the question: what if it is appropriate for someone to remove the government, but it ought not to be the military? What if military removal of the government makes subsequent democratic rule more difficult rather than less? Can we perhaps derive a practical rule that the military should never overthrow the government, no matter what, but that it may not necessarily have to continue obeying it?

Together, the findings of this literature indicate that there are a large number of factors leading to coup attempts aside from the content of the military professional ethic, and that it is not clear to what extent a change in ethic could alter or overcome those factors (e.g., a concern with organizational self-interest). On the other hand, if coups are mainly a coordination problem (Geddes 1999; Singh 2014), then the content of the professional ethic could be decisive (Kenwick 2020). More importantly for our purposes of considering an ethic that sustains democratic societies and values, coups in democracies take place only once some crisis of legitimacy is already happening, so the ethic would have to address, not normal behavior, but what to do during a crisis of democratic legitimacy.[3] This leads us to the question of how militaries behave when confronted with mass public demonstrations or protests.

---

[3] There is a growing literature on the so-called democratic coup—an idea that coups are not always bad, because they can cause a disjuncture that leads to elections and democratization (Collier 2008; Marinov and Goemans 2014; Thyne and Powell 2016). There is some evidence that this can happen, but how likely and stable a coup-produced democratic transition is, is contested (Frantz and Kendall-Taylor 2017; Tansey 2016; Derpanopoulos, Frantz, and Geddes 2016; Croissant et al. 2018). The issue is not particularly relevant for this chapter, since Thyne and Powell (2016) show that, to the extent that this happens, it happens in coups against authoritarians. In other words, coups against democratic regimes do not generally lead to better democratic regimes, so we need not consider the possibility that a coup in a democracy would be a desirable event. Marinov and Goemans (2014) do argue for the existence of a "guardian coup," in which the military "takes power from a corrupt and inept civilian administration and promises to return the country to elections after reforming the system" (803), but the examples they cite are all fairly unconsolidated democracies, and nearly all coup research indicates that even short periods of military governance are deleterious for the country's economy, civil

Behavior during Mass Protests

As noted in the introduction to this volume, one of the catalysts for the current reexamination of military professional ethics was the Arab Spring, which involved mass protests and demonstrations in several majority-Arab states in North Africa and the Middle East. The militaries in these states were all ordered by the head of state/government to deal with the protests, but they responded in very different ways. In this section, we will look at the various options militaries have under such circumstances and what factors affect how they behave. Can we determine any rules for behavior beyond simply: do not violently remove the government?

The literature on military behavior during mass demonstrations/protests notes that nondemocratic regimes nearly always at some point call on the military to contain or respond to the protests, and even democratic regimes sometimes do. Scholars are in agreement that, under such circumstances, militaries have three options: to obey their orders and suppress the protests (though they retain some control over how they behave and how much violence they exert, see Brooks 2022); to disobey their orders and passively remain "in the barracks"; or to disobey their orders and join or support the public. They could also fragment, and have different segments of the military engage in different options (Finer 1962; Bellin 2012; Croissant et al. 2018; Brooks 2022).

So, what factors determine how a military behaves under these conditions? Pion-Berlin et al. (2014) find that militaries that have (1) material grievances (organizational self-interest) against the government, (2) stronger affiliation with the public than with government elites, (3) concerns with the legality of an internal public order role (or an outright rejection of such a role), and/or (4) internal fragmentation among or within services are more likely to refuse orders and stay in the barracks, or possibly even join the protests. The affiliation with the public versus elites will derive primarily from the socioeconomic, ethnic, linguistic, or religious

---

society, and political institutions (Nordlinger 1977; Fitch 1998). On the other hand, there is evidence that military defection from a regime in the context of mass protests (as opposed to either coup or repression in obedience to the regime) can lead more reliably to democratization (Chenoweth and Stephan 2011; Lee 2014; Croissant et al. 2018).

composition of the military and will not likely be subject to military socialization efforts. Internal fragmentation is most likely to come from deliberate regime attempts to "coup-proof" (Quinlivan 1999; Boehmelt and Pilster 2015). Concerns with legality and/or role conception are potentially amenable to a professional ethic; Pion-Berlin et al. (2014) indicate that the sources of a military's role identity are primarily doctrine, training, and custom, all of which may be mutually constitutive/supportive of particular content for a professional ethic. They note that "the most prevalent causal factor ... was mission inappropriateness ... When faced with the daunting possibility of having to use force against unarmed citizens, disobedient armies could not square fulfillment of presidential orders with their perceived social responsibility to defend 'the people' or the nation" (247).

Lee's (2014) research indicates support for the structural factors noted by Pion-Berlin et al., and in other work he finds support for the military fragmentation argument (that internally fragmented militaries are more likely to defect from the regime and fail to suppress protests (Lee 2005)). Others, including Barany (2016) and Albrecht and Ohl (2016) also note the importance of military-internal cohesion and decision-making. Brooks (2022) finds support for the idea that material interests play a significant role in determining military behavior, though she argues it is not as simple as keeping the military happy and well-supplied, but also how they are kept happy and well-supplied.

Under what conditions do militaries obey orders to repress? Pion-Berlin et al. (2014) find that "obedience occurred only where material interests were satisfied and where militaries identified with government, believed internal order missions to be appropriate, followed the law, and remained unified" (246). McLauchlin (2010) and Albrecht and Ohl (2016) also find evidence of the effectiveness of ethnic stacking in keeping militaries loyal to regimes, and Bellin (2012) emphasizes that militaries under "patrimonial" systems are more likely to side with the regime than the people.[4] Makara (2013) also finds that ethnic stacking (or "exploiting communal bonds") is more likely to result in military obedience than other forms of

---

[4] While Bellin's specific concept of patrimonialism versus institutionalism has been critiqued (by inter alia Lee 2014; Barany 2016), to the extent that patrimonialism aligns with ethnic stacking, there is significant evidence for Bellin's position.

coup-proofing. Barany (2016) notes that the social distance between the military and the people demonstrating plays a significant role in whether the military obeys orders to repress, as well as whether the military feels confidence in the regime's ability and desire to protect the military's institutional interests.

So we have a fairly good picture of the structural and normative factors that matter for predicting military behavior, but this does not help us as yet with the normative question: what do we want militaries to do? The obvious but painfully unhelpful answer is: we want them to support the right side and not the wrong side. We want them to resist the government's orders to repress people who are exercising lawful rights to protest, but to obey smartly when the government is putting down a dangerous insurrection that threatens democracy. We want them to side with the people when the people are agitating for rights, but only acceptable rights, not rights to be cruel or oppressive to some group within society. Does this indicate that, in fact, we want the military to stay in the barracks in order to avoid joining the wrong side? Perhaps. But what if the regime has other security forces it can use; what if the protesters have paramilitaries and militias? Sooner or later, many militaries will face the imperative to determine which side is the right one. How will they do that?

Other Military Activity

Finally, there is the issue of military activity aside from coups or response to mass unrest. Scholars of civil-military relations have long noted that militaries and military actors can engage in a broad spectrum of behavior that can be more or less detrimental to civilian governance in general and democratic governance in particular. Huntington (1957), Finer (1962), Betts (1977), and Feaver (1996, 2003) have all argued that the problem for consolidated democracies is not that the military will be overly militaristic or unified against the civilian government in a coup or revolt, but that it will be possible for the military to exert inappropriate influence over foreign policy, budgets, and perhaps even domestic policy. Scholars of democratic breakdown and backsliding, while not generally focusing on the role of the military (Kuehn 2017: 788–9), have also noted that military activity can contribute to the erosion of democratic institutions. In this section, we examine what the empirical literature has to say about how military behavior matters for the survival and flourishing of democratic governance.

The literature on democratic breakdown is practically united in locating the cause in a loss of regime legitimacy. But that simply raises the question of how regimes lose their legitimacy. Recall that, for Augustine, a regime essentially could not lose its legitimacy; its existence justified it because it was presumed to be instituted by God. But in the present understanding of liberal theory, in which sovereignty rests in the people and therefore the people can determine the legitimacy of the regime, we must deal with this problem.

So how does a regime that came to power via democratic mechanisms embedded in an accepted legal structure, lose its legitimacy? Let us first note, again, that there is an empirically established difference between consolidated democracies and those that are still transitioning (Londregan and Poole 1990; Svolik 2015). The main difference in this particular context, however, is how quickly and how easily a regime can lose its legitimacy: consolidated democracies are far less likely to suffer this fate, and it is likely to take much longer than it would in a still-transitional state. Linz (1978) points to the interplay of political institutions and the socioeconomic system arguing that when the political institutions and parties are perceived by existing elites as not being too threatening to their interests, and when the social and economic order/distribution is perceived by the general public as basically just, the system will enjoy legitimacy and stability. When either or both of these systems is perceived as a serious threat to the interests of either group, breakdown becomes more likely. The most likely drivers of such change would of course be either significant demographic change, or an economic shock event. In a transitioning democracy where institutions are not yet well established, corruption is also a significant threat.

Linz's analysis is reconfirmed by Alexander's (2002) much more recent study, in which he shows that the political preferences of the right or conservative portion of the population are determinative for the survival of democracy, in that they must perceive the left as reliably moderate and institutions of democracy as unlikely to threaten their position or interests. This logic is one-sided for several reasons: the relevant one for our purposes is that the right has both incentives and opportunities to hedge against the possibility of a progressive takeover of democratic governance by "cultivat[ing] privileged personal and partisan ties within the military ... When in office, they reorganize[] partisan sympathizers into key military commands and perhaps purge[] supporters of left parties from throughout the state security forces ... They champion[] the budgetary resources needed to permit a politically sympathetic military to intervene effectively in political life" (Alexander 2002: 60). In short, under democracy, conservative parties and elites have incentives to be ready to "pull" the military into politics (cf. Bove, Rivero, and Ruffa 2020). Inglehart and Norris (2016: 2–5) also support this explanation, finding that anti-democratic populist parties are supported primarily on the basis of feelings of cultural threat (i.e., by groups that used to hold social and political power, but are afraid they are losing that power), and not mainly on the basis of economic deprivation.

Levitsky and Ziblatt (2019: 106) argue that a society must widely accept two norms for democratic institutions to retain their legitimacy: acceptance of political rivals as possibly undesirable but acceptable alternative leaders (as long as they abide by the law—"mutual tolerance"), and a certain amount of self-restraint exercised by policymakers to resist the temptation to increase their power by means that are technically legal but violate the spirit of the law ("institutional forbearance"). This fits in neatly with both Linz's and Alexander's arguments: if one party or faction begins to see democratic institutions as potentially allowing some party that they find unacceptable into power, they are likely to resist by attempting to block members of that group or party from participating and/or by taking over the levers of power and reducing the scope of free participation on the basis of individual equality.

Diamond (2021) argues that the "principal method of democratic regression has been ... by elected (typically populist) executives who gradually eviscerate institutional checks, political opposition, independent media, and other forces of scrutiny and resistance in civil society. Weak and declining rule of law has predisposed regimes to democratic regression, enabling ambitious rulers to hollow out political competition." He also points to economic concerns such as recession and unemployment as providing opportunities for populist leadership to accrue power to themselves without overwhelming civil resistance. In an earlier piece he argued that "for democratic structures to endure and to be worthy of endurance-they must listen to their citizens' voices, engage their participation, tolerate their protests, protect their freedoms, and respond to their needs" (Diamond 2008: 39). For democracy to survive, the demos must believe it is working. But "the demos" consists of multiple groups with potentially conflicting interests, so what this means in practice is that enough of the groups with social, economic, and political power must believe that allowing some level of uncertainty about who the governing party is and what their policies will be, will not be devastating to their interests.

In short, most democratic backsliding or breakdown appears to stem from some group (either current governing elite or populist challenge to governing elite) that feels it is losing power, using nominally legal means to consolidate their position and prevent challengers from competing effectively for power. Such challenges nearly always come from the political right, since they tend to be both more likely to be in a position of existing power and more comfortable with more authoritarian forms of governance (Alexander 2002).

The military is sometimes the aggrieved party, but as noted above, the military almost never acts to overthrow democracy (coup or protest) unless there is clear loss of legitimacy with some significant segment of the public, and unless the military identifies more closely with the protesting public than with the ruling regime and believes it can successfully act collectively. Under democratic backsliding, the military is more likely to be "pulled" into the process, and in such cases, it will be more effectively "pulled" by whichever portion of the elite/public it identifies more closely with (or it will split).

Most of the remedies for these types of concerns are thought to be found in structures of civilian control and democratic oversight, such as civilian jurisdiction over military crimes, parliamentary review of actions and control of budgets, civilian ministers or secretaries above all uniformed personnel in the chain of command, laws establishing the allowable uses of the military, and the like (Nordlinger 1977; Stepan 1988; Fitch 1998; Feaver 2003; Cohn 2011; Kyle and Reiter 2021; White 2023). Other useful counterweights are the availability of civilian defense experts, to improve oversight and offer alternative views (Stepan 1988: 133; Fitch 1998; Cottey, Edmunds, and Forster 2002); a clear mission and sufficient budget (Fitch 1998); an appropriate professional ethic, inculcated primarily through a system of professional education, as well as doctrine, training, and organizational culture (Huntington 1957; Janowitz 1960; Stepan 1988; Fitch 1998); and finally, effective and legitimate democratic governance (Fitch 1998; Cottey, Edmunds, and Forster 2002; Cohn 2011).

The Framing Questions

In the two previous chapters we have asked a series of questions—first of Augustinian theory, then of democratic theories. Here we will not ask about the primary political value or the legitimation of violence in society, but we will take another look at the questions regarding how to resolve the puzzle of simultaneous military effectiveness and obedience, as well as the role of the soldier in society.

In this chapter, we have encountered multiple theorists whose primary concern was to settle the question of how to achieve simultaneous military effectiveness and civil or democratic control. The consensus view is that it is fairly easy to achieve either one or the other, but to achieve both, one needs effective institutions of governance, some mechanism reducing preference discrepancy between the military and policy leadership, and some ethical disposition on the part of the military that causes them to believe they ought not to act in certain ways (cf. Cohn 2011). Points of disagreement lie mainly in which methods to use to reduce preference discrepancy, and in what, precisely, the ethic should teach military personnel not to do.

What have we learned from this literature about the role of the soldier in society?

Soldier as Politician. Nearly all of this literature indicates that military members should not take active part in the electoral struggle for power in the polity or in the making of laws. Even those like Cohen and Sarkesian, who argue for politically educated and savvy military officers, do not advocate that those officers should be competing at the polls for political office, or debating in a public forum over the merits of various policies. Certainly, none of this literature indicates an acceptance of any policymaking role for military leadership outside of "military issues"—that is, where they have supposed expertise. In this sense, these scholars all share a more liberal than civic republican concept of democracy. The empirical literature indicates that having uniformed or recently retired military officers in positions of policy/political authority is associated with more risk of military intervention in politics.

Soldier as Advisor. Here is where we see the clearest distinction between the Huntingtonian tradition and the others: some argue that military advisors should serve merely as technicians and consider only their functional expertise in their advice to policymakers. In this view, the policymakers explain their political goals, the military advisors explain which military options are available to them, the policymakers choose from among the options, and the officers then salute and obey, regardless of their assessment of the wisdom of the course of action. Others insist that this is not only unrealistic, but undesirable, in that it leads to bad strategy and bad policy. These scholars argue that military advisors and policymakers must be engaged in an ongoing dialogue to try to understand one another's interests and limits; that the military leadership must have some concept of and respect for the policymaker's political concerns, and that the policymaker must in turn understand and respect the officers' organizational, moral, and logistical concerns. Nearly all of this literature accepts without question the idea that military officers are expert in some sense. Those on the Huntingtonian side embody a slightly more liberal concept, that democratic legitimacy outweighs expertise (though Huntington himself did not think this—he argued that, to the extent the policymaker and the military leadership disagreed, the policymakers should shift their beliefs and preferences toward those of the military). Those on the Sarkesian-Cohen side trend somewhat more to the civic republican view that it is more important to get good policy than to have pure process.

Soldier as Enforcer. While both Augustine and democratic theory indicated that, to the extent some kind of enforcement of laws was necessary, there was no particular reason it should not be done by militaries, this turns out to be one of the most controversial aspects in this literature. A majority of scholars, both normative and empirical, argue that it is centrally important for militaries to have purely external, defensive role-conceptions; otherwise they will be much more likely to interfere in the political life of society. A minority argue that military interference in politics does not follow necessarily from an internal role conception, nor does an external role-conception guarantee noninterference, and that we should consider how these role conceptions interact with other factors. In general, most authors recognize that the military will nearly always be the enforcer of last resort, so we cannot assume away the question of how they should behave under such circumstances. It is not whether they have a conception of internal security and order at all, but what that conception is; particularly what their relationship is to the public.

Soldier as Citizen. There are not many theorists left who believe that military personnel ought to be so removed from politics as not to vote or take part in the general activities of citizenship. While some (in the Huntingtonian tradition) believe that military professionalism requires them to have a clearly illiberal ethos, emphasizing collective identity, subordination to hierarchy and authority, and coercive problem-solving, they do not generally think they ought to be cut off from society or disenfranchised. On the other hand, many (in the Janowitzean tradition) would argue that it is important that members of the military be as closely integrated with society as possible, including mirroring their demographics and their values. Thus all agree that military personnel should enjoy the basic status as citizens, but they disagree on the extent to which they should be integrated into the political life of society.[5] We know from the empirical literature that the extent to which the military—and different groups within it—identify with the people versus the elites will have a significant impact on how the military interprets its duties in a crisis.

Conclusions

While the normative theorists of civil-military relations all agree on the importance of a professional ethic for the health of democratic governance, they have not found a consensus on what the content of that ethic should be.[6]

---

[5]Note that we have not dealt with those militaries made up largely of non-citizens, such as those in several Persian Gulf states or in many other states in the centuries before the twentieth. This is an important subject, but one that is beyond our scope here.
[6]Stepan (1988: 13) notes that whether "professionalism" helps or hurts democratic governance depends largely on its content.

The empirical theorists have identified the factors that make militaries more or less likely to intervene in politics—via coup, response to protest, or other less overt means—but have not solved the question of whether it is always necessarily bad for democracy for militaries to obey (or not), or to intervene (or not) in specific ways. In general, we want a military that is loyal and obedient to the government, but what if that government is committing human rights abuses, abusing its power, or undermining the system itself? Would we rather the military remained neutral? If not, on what ethical or empirical basis should they determine their course of action?

If we take the position that it is always better for militaries to refrain from interfering, we are faced with the problem that structural factors will almost certainly not be able to produce such an outcome. If militaries are "coup-proofed"[7] to prevent them from overthrowing the government, they will more likely identify with the government in case of crisis or protests.[8] If the military is designed to be deeply integrated with society, it will be more likely to disobey the government when there is a legitimacy crisis. This means that the content of the military ethic—the thing telling them what is right and wrong in a given situation—would be critical.

While loyalty to the legal regime is undoubtedly important, major concerns arise as to how far that loyalty ought to extend when the regime itself is acting questionably, and which actors have the authority and legitimacy to judge when the regime has crossed a line. On the other hand, while loyalty to a concept of the people or the nation is desirable, that can become problematic when the

---

[7]Coup-proofing techniques include the so-called ethnic stacking, parallel military structures, pervasive security or intelligence services, satisfaction of material demands, or professionalization (Quinlivan 1999). Ethnic stacking does not have to be on the basis of ethnicity; it refers to the practice of ensuring that the officer corps overwhelmingly identifies with the ruling party, whether that is via ethnicity, language, religion, kinship, or socio-economic class. Parallel military structures refer to the practice of fragmenting the military into different groups, especially when one group is small but significantly privileged over others and can serve as a home guard to the ruling elite in case of rebellion by the larger rank and file. There is significant evidence in all of the literature we have discussed that ethnic stacking, parallel structures, pervasive security forces, and satisfaction of material interests are fairly effective at keeping a military from engaging in coup, but they also heighten the likelihood a military would obey orders to repress peaceful protesters.

[8]This is not a determinative judgment, merely a probabilistic one. See Brooks (2013).

military interprets what is right for the nation differently from the way the government interprets it (Robinson, Cohn, and Margulies 2021). This review of the empirical literature has yielded no list of acceptable and unacceptable behaviors, because the desirability of the behaviors depends on the values at stake, who is threatening those values, and who is competent to determine whether the threat is significant enough to constitute the kind of emergency that overrides the normal rules.

It is to the contents of an appropriate professional ethic that we turn in the final chapter.

5

A Democratic Military Professionalism?

We now come to the most difficult part of our inquiry. Can we discern an ethic that can serve military professionals in democratic societies, to help them determine right and wrong in situations of social and political tension? Can we help them have a clearer idea of their duty in the midst of a political crisis? We are concerned here with crises of democratic legitimacy, however they may arise.

For Augustine, as we saw, this was a concern he never addressed explicitly, finding it sufficient to implore soldiers, like everyone else, to obey the authority over them. But this did not provide a truly comprehensive ethic; he left open to question what one should do when the authority contradicted the laws, and he never explained which of God's laws one should follow in spite of authority and which one should ignore because ordered to do so.

The democratic theorists were generally also not concerned with situating the military or other bureaucratic or expert actors in their society. They had enough difficulty defining the parameters of the society and determining whether legitimacy arose more from procedure or outcome. In short, they left the question of legitimate authority as one that can be solved only by specific groups of people at specific times, and which must be constantly revisited. They left us with some ideas—some conflicting, some complementary—about what a democratic society should value and seek to preserve, and order was only one possible value among many.

The civil-military relations scholars, both normative and empirical, left us with the distinct impression that an ethic is critical to healthy civil-military relations, but no clear guidance on what the content of that ethic should be. Whatever it is, it must deal with the questions of how to achieve both military effectiveness and obedience, what the military's concept should be of its own nature and role in society, and what the nature is of the entity to which it has sworn allegiance.

The chapter proceeds as follows: we first note the fact that some form of ethic of self-control or self-restraint is indispensable from every perspective we have explored. This leads us through a discussion of the idea of professions, the idea of professional ethics, and the specific case of militaries. We then summarize the moral and ethical ideas we have collected thus far and, finally, consider whether an alternative, democratic military ethic, is conceivable.

The Centrality of Self-Restraint

The literature on democratic civil-military relations indicates that the key to achieving both effectiveness and obedience is to convince military personnel that they occupy a specific role in society; one that requires them to be both competent and self-restrained. In Huntington's account, this is conceived of as military "professionalism." If officers believed themselves to be "professionals," then they would believe all the things necessary to keep them both competent and subordinate. Huntington defined a profession as having expertise, a corporate identity, and a belief in the need to use their expertise for the service of some good beyond themselves (responsibility) (Huntington 1957: 8–18; see also Snider 2015). Countless commentators since have noted that Huntington's definition of professionalism is somewhat tautological (see e.g., Feaver 2003; Fitch 1998), in that it assumes that subordination to civilian policy control is definitionally part of the professional ethic, rather than acknowledging the need to define a content for the ethic. Nearly everyone who has tried to rectify this problem, however, has started from Huntington's definition of a profession and his fundamental assumption that military officers constitute a profession.

Professions and the Professional

It may be worthwhile to explore this concept further. Sociologists have long tried to figure out what people mean when they call something a profession. The term "professional" has been contrasted with "amateur" (e.g., Janowitz 1960: 6), with "commercial" (Parsons 1937, 1939), with "trade/craft," with "part-time/hobby," and more. And it can of course have more than one meaning depending on the context. Early on, there was a movement among sociologists (with its high point in the 1950s and 1960s) to define professions via ideal-type (the "taxonomic" approach, see Saks 2012). Huntington falls squarely within this group. But this approach was later criticized by the whole field from various perspectives, some of which noted that the taxonomic approach failed to acknowledge the sociopolitical processes involved in identifying some occupations/groups as professions/professionals, and others of which noted that the idea that specific knowledge/education was what separated professions from not-professions was very problematic.

The taxonomic approach attempted to define professions by a list of characteristics that divided them from not-professions. All agreed that what was at issue were occupations, and that some occupations were in fact professions and some were not. They disagreed on whether this was a dichotomous situation or a spectrum, and also on whether or not something could become a profession, or whether the nature was static (Saks 2012). Taxonomic arguments tended to center around the ideas of a special body of knowledge that required study and theorizing rather than just practice, a certain amount of authority/autonomy based on the fact that no lay person could understand their competency or rules, and a certain service orientation, based on the facts that the society needed their competency to thrive, and that they (the professionals) engaged in this occupation primarily (though not exclusively) for non-self-interested reasons (Parsons 1937, 1939; Greenwood 1957; Wilensky 1964). Huntington summarized this in the claim that professions were characterized (and differentiated from not-professions) by their aspects of expertise, corporateness, and responsibility.

Also necessary, as derived from these characteristics, was a professional ethic: a set of norm or value statements arrived at by considering what roles the professionals had to play, and how they should relate to their clients (those relying directly on their expertise) and to one another, in order to maintain society's trust and thereby their own autonomy. Janowitz (1960: 6) also used this approach, defining a profession as a group possessing specialized expertise, a sense of group identity, and a system of internal/self-administration (sometimes supported by the power of the state), and said that these things "impl[y] the growth of a body of ethics and standards of performance." In short, many of these scholars assumed that because professions would need an ethical code to protect their authority, legitimacy, and effectiveness, they would automatically develop them. We now realize, of course, that the content of a professional ethic is not automatically appropriate, and needs to be carefully constructed.

Sociology as a field moved away from the taxonomic approach, and has long since recognized that the category of "profession" is far less objective and more sociopolitically contested than the taxonomists believed. This is where the concept of "professionalization" comes from—the idea that some occupation that was not a profession can take on aspects of a profession, that individuals within a group may become more professional over time, or even that whether something is a profession or not has little to do with its objective characteristics and everything to do with how effectively it can convince the society (and the legislature) to grant it a measure of autonomy and prestige (Saks 2012). A number of scholars have questioned the extent to which the military is, in fact, a profession, including noting that it may be aspiring to the idea more than embodying it (Shanks Kaurin 2018b), arguing that it lacks a universal ethos (Ingesson 2018) or arguing that there is no such thing as "military expertise," broadly conceived (Cohn 2018).

Fitch (1998: 5) offers a particularly damning critique of "professionalism" (as defined by Huntingtonian loyalty ethics) as a self-serving political choice by elites: "Classical professionalism's emphasis on loyalty and subordination to the state and its opposition to political involvements reinforced the power of the incumbent state authorities and inhibited political alliances between military officers and civilian groups opposed to the oligarchical regime." Having an ethic that stresses that the military stay out of politics automatically reinforces whatever the political constellation is at the time. This is probably good for order and stability, but not necessarily for rights or justice. Fitch describes how, in societies where the wealthy merchants were able to establish control over the levers of government, they encouraged a classical version of the professional ethic. But

> where the export oligarchy was not able to establish a clear hegemony, civilian elites often opted for a model of civil-military relations that allowed *conditional* military allegiance to civilian authority ... To overcome professional resistance to political involvements, civilian appeals were coached [*sic*] in terms of a higher loyalty—to the patria (fatherland) and to protection of "national interests"—superseding obedience to the president. (Fitch 1998: 6)

Fitch's account indicates that the "obedient apolitical military" model is really possible only under a hegemonic regime widely accepted by the population. The presence of significant political struggle will make that nearly impossible; adding in the democratic concept of continuous change in regime and policy, "apolitical" soon becomes "amoral."

In his investigation of the process of professionalization, Wilensky (1964) looked empirically at the historical development of several occupations he considered to be either well-established or newly minted professions. He argued that there were several common steps, one of the last of which was the development of an explicit code of ethics for the profession. It may come as a surprise that this code of ethics—treated as central to the identity of the profession by most taxonomists—came fairly late in the development of the professions Wilensky examined. His observation does, however, help to explain why the US Army could still be criticized as late as at least 2010 for its lapses in ethical judgment and behavior thus: "In part, the reason for lapses and inconsistencies is that the [professional] ethic has never been clearly and succinctly codified" (Moten 2010: 19).

But before we examine the specific military ethic, let us ask, for a moment, why professions need an ethic, what purpose the ethic is supposed to serve, and whether the military profession (assuming for the moment that it is a profession) has any special needs for its ethic to address, that other professions do not.

Professional Ethics

Applied or practical ethics are sets of standards that tell people how to behave in specific types of situations (Snider 2015: 16–17). Medical ethics, legal ethics, business ethics, and so on, are all names for specific applied ethics. In other words, when we talk about "professional" ethics, we are talking about how members of a particular profession discuss how to behave rightly and wrongly in the context of their profession (Snider 2015; Shanks Kaurin 2018a).

Monopolies, powers, privileges, and authority can all be abused, so professions must have a code of ethics. According to Greenwood (1957: 50), this code of ethics functions primarily in two ways: as a guide to the behavior of professionals in order to maintain the reputation and trustworthiness of the group and as a pledge to the community that they can trust the group. French (2017) notes that this latter function is particularly important for militaries (or warriors), as they are likely to have engaged in behavior that would normally be considered transgressive of social norms and need some signifier that their own societies can trust them.

In one of the earlier treatments, Parsons (1939) identifies the core elements of a profession as universalism (serving any and all clients regardless of their particular characteristics—including the ability to pay), disinterestedness (doing a service rather than serving self-interest), rationality (critical self-reflection and updating of knowledge), and functional specificity (sticking to one's own sphere of competence). These certainly constitute moral values that could form the basis of a professional ethic. Greenwood (1957: 50–1) adds to these the moral values/expectations of cooperativeness with colleagues (advances in knowledge are shared quickly so everyone can benefit), equalitarianism with colleagues (recognition based purely on performance at the task), and supportiveness of colleagues (avoid undermining fellow members of the profession and sustain their authority when threatened). Greenwood argues that,

> [a customer's] freedom of decision rests upon the premise that he has the capacity to appraise his own needs and to judge the potential of the service or of the commodity to satisfy them … In a professional relationship, however, the professional dictates what is good or evil for the client, who has no choice but to accede to professional judgment. Here the premise is that,

because he lacks the requisite theoretical background, the client cannot diagnose his own needs or discriminate among the range of possibilities for meeting them. Nor is the client considered able to evaluate the caliber of the professional service he receives ... The client's subordination to professional authority invests the professional with a monopoly of judgment. (48)

This level of dependency between the client and the professional is part of what necessitates that the professional have an ethic—not just a morality, which may be personal, but a code that has been reflected upon and discussed amongst the community of practice as appropriate to their roles and positions (Shanks Kaurin 2018a). Greenwood goes on to note: "The professional's authority, however, is not limitless; its function is confined to those specific spheres within which the professional has been educated ... The professional cannot prescribe guides for facets of the client's life where his theoretical competence does not apply" (48). So part of the ethic involves a certain level of honesty and humility about not issuing authoritative statements on things in which the professional holds no special expertise.

Military Professional Ethics

Again, assuming for now that there is such a thing as a military profession, military professional ethics are about how members of the military profession (and those who think about and study that profession) think about and discuss how to behave rightly in the situations they are likely to find themselves in as members of that profession.

The German military has dealt with this problem more thoughtfully than those of most other Western states, having had to confront the question of when exactly the military servicemember should determine not to follow orders on the grounds of their illegitimacy rather than their illegality. Their solution was a concept called *Innere Fuehrung*:[1] conceived of as "socialization, as

---

[1] The Germans translate this as "leadership development and civic education"; "In 1982, Graf von Baudissin—the father of Innere Führung—defined its general sense as follows: 'Innere Führung is military leadership with special consideration of the individual and social aspects of the person.'" (Bernzen, Peddinghaus, and Sieger

active shaping, and hence 'raising' to become a responsible citizen in uniform, who is bound by the common good and does not share a vision of the state within a state ... it describes the identity of a responsible and constructively critical soldier in the 21st century" (Bernzen, Peddinghaus, and Sieger 2016). Hartman (2016) explains that part of *Innere Fuehrung* was the expansion of the concept of mission command beyond the purely technical military realm:

> Leading by mission was understood not just purely in military terms but also politically. It was supposed to be not simply a matter of carrying out a military order in the most effective way possible, but also of considering beforehand whether the likely outcome of one's action in fact served the political purpose. In this way, the soldier came to share responsibility for the political objectives that were to be achieved. The concept of leading by mission or mission-type tactics was therefore expanded to become leading with a politically justified mission, a "mission strategy." Politics is therefore an indispensable element of soldierly professionalism. (Hartman 2016: 23–4)

So the Germans focused their military professional ethic on preventing the military from being used by an immoral or criminal regime; their touchstone traumatic experience was the loss of democracy and slide into war at least partially through a military that viewed obeying orders (and maintaining conservative political primacy (Hett 2018)) as its prime value. This is the opposite solution to that promoted by Huntington (notable particularly because Huntington recognized the dilemma in which Wehrmacht officers found themselves, but somehow continued to advocate for the same approach they had).

This approach is appropriate in the German context, and it could be argued that such "politicization" of the military and of military personnel is less threatening in that context because of the institutional and sociopolitical weakness of the German military.

2016), but it is literally translated as "internal leadership"—referring to the idea that the German soldier or officer must not merely obey orders, but have an internal compass, as well, that aids in evaluating those orders. See also Dörfler-Dierken (2005).

But what about in the United States, or any other country where the military is highly respected, well-funded, and influential?

In the 2010s, the US Army (in particular) sponsored a number of studies into the idea of the Army Ethic, apparently hoping to clarify and codify it. Moten (2010: 20–1) suggested a potential codification that basically followed Hartle's (2004: 73–4) principles of the professional ethic: (1) service to country and defense of the Constitution; (2) honorable conduct as members of a profession whose "integrity, loyalty, and moral and physical courage are exemplary"; (3) maintenance of the highest level of competency in relevant skills/knowledge; (4) responsibility for actions; (5) "Promote and safeguard, within the context of mission accomplishment, the welfare of their subordinates as persons, not merely as [service-members]"; (6) obedience to the laws of war and of the country; and (7) "Conform strictly to the principle that subordinates the military to civilian authority. They do not involve themselves or their subordinates in domestic politics beyond the exercise of basic civil rights."

These seem indisputable, but the problem is that they assume the existence of a basic consensus on moral and political values; they do not give guidance on how to behave in a context of significant discord or change. What if "basic civil rights" are a hotly contested issue? What if—as the Germans recognize—there can be distance between what is legal and what is legitimate? What if members of the military begin to question whether the process they are sworn to uphold is producing legitimate outcomes?

Moten (2010) argues that,

> The ethics of a professional officer serving this [US] constitutional democracy have evolved toward an understanding of the military's place in and duty to society, a high level of professional expertise, a sense of military service as a full-time occupation and a long-term calling, a subordination to duly elected and appointed civil authority, an ethos of positive and responsible leadership of subordinates, and a moral-ethical compass fixed on the laws of war and the Constitution. (19)

But is this enough? We have seen in past chapters that the problem lies precisely in the failure of an ethic to specify how to act when these vague values are in conflict.

Martin Dempsey, former chairman of the US Joint Chiefs of Staff wrote,

> Our profession is distinguished from others in society because of our expertise in the justified application of lethal military force and the willingness of those who serve to die for our Nation. Our profession is defined by our values, ethics, standards, code of conduct, skills and attributes. As volunteers, our sworn duty is to the Constitution. Our status as a profession is granted by those whom we are accountable to, our civilian authority, and the American people. (2010: 4)

This is, if possible, even more vague. Of more concern, however, are the clear assumptions that this profession is somehow specially—almost sacredly—connected to The Nation, and that the Constitution is a clear and self-evident document on which there is societal consensus.

In 2017, Swain and Pierce released a new edition of *The Armed Forces Officer*, in which the then-CJCS Dunford wrote, "this new edition … articulates the ethical and moral underpinnings at the core of our profession." Their version of the ethic emphasized that the officer's commission and oath signified a commitment to service to the nation as a whole—implying a consideration of the common or public good rather than the good of a particular political party or other subgroup in society; a commitment to obey lawful orders—implying much less room for individual critical analysis or conscience than the German model; a commitment to act honorably and competently, with integrity, justice, and fairness towards all subordinates. They note that S. L. A. Marshall, when he wrote the first edition of the book, held fidelity to be the prime virtue.

But again, these unobjectionable values provide no guidance under conditions of disagreement, discord, or contestation. What if the question of who constitutes "the nation" is contested? Of what constitutes "service" or the public good? What if laws are in conflict or the public is openly questioning the legitimacy of the law and main institutions of law? Fidelity to what? What happens when there is no fundamental societal consensus on morality, values, or governance?

Robinson, Cohn, and Margulies (2021) attempt to characterize the various strands of loyalty that may pull a military service-member in different directions. They argue that these include a loyalty to the authority structure (obedience to authorities), to the operational imperative (technical competence), to the institutions of government (obedience to laws and regulations), to their own subordinates, to their personal moral convictions, to the support of liberal democratic governance, and to a "professional ethos" (Robinson, Cohn, and Margulies 2021: 66–75). The authors do not provide any solution to the problems they identify but argue that all of these loyalties can theoretically conflict with one another, and that it is imperative that a military ethic provide some guidance on how to resolve such conflicts.

Constructive Deviance

Clausewitz argues that one cannot be an expert at war, one can only become a better judge of the situation (Cohn 2018). Shanks Kaurin (2018b; 2020; inter alia) argues that judgment honed through experience is essential to an appropriate understanding of obedience as negotiation. Robinson, Cohn, and Margulies (2021) argue that military personnel will almost inevitably find themselves in situations where rules or values are in conflict. In the literature on organizational behavior, this is called constructive deviance, variously defined as "intentional behaviors that depart from the norms of a referent group in honorable ways" (Spreitzer and Sonenshein 2003: 9), or "behaviors that depart from the norms of the reference group such that they benefit the reference group and conform to hypernorms" (Vadera, Pratt, and Mishra 2013: 1223). This is a helpful concept for us, as it implies that a military servicemember may depart from the norms of the military ethic (whether it is a profession or not) if it is done in a way that is in service to more fundamental norms—perhaps those of the larger referent group, that is, society. But this brings us right back to the problem of what to do when that larger referent group does not have consensus on the meaning or hierarchy of various moral and political values. It puts us right back in the trap identified in Chapter 4, of militaries who see themselves as guardians of some concept of the nation that transcends "politics."

Indeed, this problem of the military's proper sphere of expertise is one of the problems with thinking of military service per se as a profession. People in militaries certainly may develop specific forms of expertise, in, say, nuclear engineering, or logistics. But the idea that there is a body of expertise that all military officers (and probably noncommissioned officers (NCOs), too) develop; the idea that the "management of violence" is a body of knowledge that can be taught in schools is highly questionable. Clausewitz certainly would not have called it an expertise—he never uses a term that could be translated as such in *On War* (Cohn 2018: 77). In many militaries, in fact, the personnel system is designed specifically to avoid having individuals become experts in specific areas. They are instead expected to become generalists; by doing many different jobs as they advance, they are expected to develop a good general sense of how their part of the military works. In terms of their role as advisors to policymakers, their "expertise" consists primarily in understanding how the military organization and its components works, but this is an expertise developed more by experience than by study.

One of the central dilemmas of officer-level professional military education is determining precisely what it ought to teach. Officers will learn doctrine, they will learn some military history, they will learn some basics of military organization and functions, they may learn something about the policy processes in their country, they will learn relevant law and regulations, but what exactly is their expertise? The point is not that military officers and NCOs have no knowledge or skills, but that it is very difficult to define the contents of the "body of knowledge" that is supposed to constitute "military expertise." This becomes important, then, when people are trying to determine, according to their professional ethic, what does and what does not fall into their realm of competence. They may possess the requisite humble character, but may draw the lines differently from others in their peer group, from specific policymakers, and from society in general.

What We Have Discovered Thus Far

Augustine's Military Ethic

Prime political value: order/authority
Legitimization of violence: if ordered by authority (needful to maintain order and create righteous people)

Control and effectiveness: obey authority, do your job well
Soldier as politician: obey the law
Soldier as advisor: be honest and competent, but also obey authority
Soldier as enforcer: obey the law and authority
Soldier as citizen: obey the law and authority

Liberal Democracy's Military Ethic

Prime political value: individual liberty of the person (primarily negative liberty)

Legitimization of violence: government has authority to use violence to enforce rules (but only with proportionality), protect persons/property, defend the polity, possibly wage aggressive war …

Control and effectiveness: people should fulfill contracts

Soldier as politician: military as organization should not be involved in political competition; individuals may, but only if they dissociate from the military

Soldier as advisor: military should provide technical advice but recognize that the only legitimate authority for policymaking is the elected official and their decisions prevail in every instance; no organizational considerations should interfere with or trump elected political discretion

Soldier as enforcer: obey laws and political authority

Soldier as citizen: enjoy full participatory rights as individuals

Civic Republicanism's Military Ethic

Prime political value: liberty of the individual (positive liberty in the form of active participation and development of civic virtue), ergo, participation

Legitimization of violence: government has authority to use violence to enforce rules (but if a lot of rule-breaking is occurring, that's a failing society), and to defend the polity from external threats (but in a limited and proportional way)

Control and effectiveness: serve and obey out of civic obligation and virtue; it is implied that these motivations will make people effective soldiers

Soldier as politician: if virtuous and wise, then the soldier (officer) ought to lend these assets to the community; the military member ought not, however, to participate in politics in the service of their organization or factional interests—this view is least friendly to a "professionalized" military

Soldier as advisor: use expertise and wisdom for common good; avoid organizational or corporate interests influencing advice

Soldier as enforcer: fulfill the will of the community and enforce its rules

Soldier as citizen: enjoy and exercise full participatory rights as individuals

A Pragmatic (Democratic) Military Ethic

Prime political value: maintaining democratic governance

Legitimization of violence: contested

Control and effectiveness: a military ethic of subordination and obedience is important, but so are institutional structures that limit people's ability to disobey

Soldier as politician: members of the military should not serve in elected or appointed positions (except insofar as appointed positions are subordinate to elected or appointed civilians); they should have no influence over policy outside their own sphere of expertise, and their autonomy within their sphere should be limited by structure and extensive oversight. Recently retired career officers should hold themselves to these same standards voluntarily.

Soldier as advisor: two schools of thought:

Huntingtonian: military should provide technical military advice, only, no political analysis or recommendations; they have no competence in determining the good of the political unit

Janowitzean/Sarkesian/Cohen: military officers should develop political acumen sufficient to help them participate in a productive strategic dialogue with elected and appointed officials, working together toward a consensus understanding of the good of the political unit

Soldier as enforcer: if it can be avoided, soldiers should not engage in domestic law enforcement except as a last resort, in order to help them stay out of political questions and avoid having to think of their fellow citizens as "enemies"

Soldier as citizen: two schools of thought:

Huntingtonian: members of the military must maintain a separate and higher ethos than the general public, illiberal and focused on technical competence. They may vote, but should engage in other political activity as little as possible, including dialogue

Janowitzean: members of the military ought to be well-integrated with society, understanding, respecting, and mirroring society's values and demographics. They should participate in the political life of society, but from a place of equality, not superiority

An Alternative?

Many codifications of military ethics appear to take a virtue ethics approach—emphasizing the moral character of the individual—and that if they cultivate their own virtuousness, they will make good decisions in difficult situations. The key concepts in virtue ethics (relevant to this discussion) are excellence (*arete*) and moral wisdom (*phronesis*). Excellence is about conscious practice of virtues for their own sake; *phronesis* is developed as wisdom or judgment that comes with experience. Virtue ethics does not actually require an explicit code of behavior, because it is about character rather than specific action.[2] In fact, a major objection to

---

[2]Although Shanks Kaurin (2018b) argues that the *right application of any code* requires *phronesis*, or judgment/sensitivity derived from experience. I.e., even codified ethics require practice and experience to be carried out reliably.

virtue ethics is its inability to provide specific action guidance; this is not entirely fair, as it does indicate that in any given situation one should do what is virtuous (what is honest, charitable, courageous, etc.), but that is not helpful for a code of professional ethics unless the concrete meaning of these terms is further specified by that profession. Virtue ethics have dilemmas in them—situations where two virtues point to different behavior. How should such be resolved? In virtue ethics, the resolution comes through *phronesis*—anyone with sufficient practical wisdom will understand how to rank the virtues or rules involved. Again, though, this is not helpful in a situation where the basic meaning of virtues may be contested, or there may be no consensus on the values to which they should be applied.

In fact, the lack of guidance provided by virtue ethics (and the practical difficulty of ensuring that everyone in the institution is in fact virtuous) means that, while using the language of virtue, military professional ethics are strongly deontological. Deontological ethics are those in which acting in accordance with the rules defines ethical behavior. This is a concept of what we ought to do as opposed to who we ought to be. Another way of thinking about it is that it is more important that we do what is "right" (according to the rules) than that we do what is "good" (according to some overarching concept of good). This is fundamentally the idea that whether an order is lawful or not is the only consideration, *not* whether it is legitimate. Under this conception of a professional ethic, it is not the province of the technical expert to determine whether the ends are appropriate, only to follow the code. Deontological ethics can also run into dilemmas and also tend to resolve them by implying that the rules have some hierarchy, and practical wisdom allows the individual to know which rule ought to take precedence in a given situation.

By now, the parallels between civic republican democracy and virtue ethics and between liberal/procedural democracy and deontological ethics should be clear. As with the democratic theories, the ethical systems meet and mingle in reality.

But there are other ethical systems, and these also find their way into the discussion. Utilitarian ethics requires us to consider not just the virtue of the self who does the action, or the rule-abidingness of the action, but the immediate and follow-on effects of the action: will this action produce good or bad effects? We see this form of ethical reasoning in Feaver's (2003) imperative for the military officer to protect the civil-military relationship, while also endeavoring to obey the principal's directives, and in the legal and ethical imperative for service-members to avoid acting in a way that "brings discredit" upon the organization. There is also an ethics of care, which emphasizes the moral value of interpersonal relationships and care as a characteristic. This may seem out of place in a discussion of military ethics, but we see it embodied both in the idea of the almost parental relationship of a commanding officer to their subordinates and in the insistence of most militaries in democratic contexts that taking care of their people is critical to their health and effectiveness as an organization.

Shanks Kaurin (2018b) argues that the military does not constitute a settled profession, but a community aspiring to the meaning and status of profession. If this is the case, she argues, then "the community must continually reflect on its profession; discuss the identity, function, and the ethical standards that go with that identity" (14). This is analogous to the concept of democratic governance needing to be constantly reconstituted. In theory, these are excellent visions of societies that are open and willing to talk about difficult issues of identity, value, and meaning; but in practice, this puts people in any given specific situation in a very difficult position. It means there is no anchor (cf. MacIntyre 2015: 12).

This, then, is the situation in which military people find themselves when one rule tells them that they must be politically sterile or neutral, and another rule tells them they must take care of their subordinates in situations of societal racism, or maintain good order and discipline in situations of mass public demonstrations, or defend the Constitution in situations where the meaning of the Constitution is contested. Multiple potential primary values to be defended, no settled understanding of the contents of a professional ethic, no consensus on the nature or existence of a profession, and not even a consensus on which model of ethical thinking should take precedence.

In short, it does not seem possible to create an ethic that will serve any given military in any given democracy, for too much is contingent.

Conclusions

The problem with all these lists of values (honor, integrity, loyalty, duty, obedience, courage) is that they never specify what exactly these things mean (loyalty to what/whom?) and thus leave open the possibility that significant differences of ethos are being papered over by superficial agreement on vague terms.

MacIntyre argues that all virtues are contextual: "Everything turns on what goods are at stake … To be courageous is not only for an agent to risk or to endure dangers and harms, but to do so in a way and to an extent that is proportionate to the goods at stake in that agent's situation … one cannot be courageous unless one has, and exercises, the ability to identify the goods at stake in particular situations" (2015: 4). Practical wisdom, prudence, experience, judgment: whatever name it is given, it is critical to judging what is right or wrong for a given individual in a given context: "Knowing what rules to apply and how to apply them is itself an exercise of prudence and not of rule-following" (MacIntyre 2015: 9).

6

Conclusion

It seems we have determined that, from a normative perspective, we have a problem of infinite regression. To have a military that is both militarily effective and subordinate, it must exert self-restraint, via some set of ethics or norms that explain the right and wrong ways to use its coercive capabilities. That set of ethics, to maintain a proper relationship between the policymakers in a democratic society and the military leadership, must be capable of constant self-reflection and change, and must involve some concept of political acumen and behavior. A simple imperative to "stay out of politics" is strategically problematic at best and counterproductive at worst, allowing military officers to remove problematic politicians from their position "above" the political fray.

But if that set of ethics involves some political role for the military, and some need to be politically informed and astute, then we have a new problematique: how to have a military savvy enough to participate appropriately in the policymaking process and be active in the democratic endeavor, but not interested in using their savvy to serve their own interests or undermine the system? Again, the normative answer must include some form of ethic that teaches the officer the right and wrong ways to use his or her political acumen. In every step, we are asking members of the military to acquire skills and capabilities, but to use them only for good, not for ill. This would already be a great deal to ask of any human, but when there is no consensus on what counts as good or ill, and when it is empirically difficult to distinguish them, we have gone well beyond reasonable expectations.

In short, there is no specific ethic that we could develop that would resolve these problems once and for all. So long as the meaning and structure of democratic legitimacy remain contested—indeed, so long as democracy remains a system that must be continuously constituted and reconstituted by the ongoing actions of its members—we will not be able to formulate a specific ethic that will tell members of the military the right and wrong of a given situation. The right and wrong in a given situation may be undergoing evolution, themselves, or the hierarchy of rights may be changing.

Not only this, but it is undesirable from both a social and a political perspective to expect military personnel to be superhumanly virtuous. This is not least because the more they are held up as superhumanly virtuous the more they will believe it of themselves, and the more likely they will be to take political judgments upon themselves or disdain the will of the public. As we saw in the preceding chapters, one of the mistakes a society ought to try to avoid is putting the military on a pedestal—whether it be for virtue, exclusive expertise, or selflessness. One marker of healthy civil-military relations is mutual respect between society and the military, not one-sided hero worship.

In practical, empirical terms, societies will always need to use a combination of methods to reduce the severity of the civil-military problematique; relying on a professional ethic alone will never suffice. Which combination of methods is best will vary by society and context.

Finally, we come to the fact that the military cannot and should not be looked to for the rescue of crumbling democracy. While there may be instances where militaries play a constructive role, it is almost never in the best long-term interests of society. Democracy saved by a military often loses its democratic character over the longer run. I am not speaking here of militaries remaining loyal to a democratically legitimated leader who must fight a civil war against undemocratic forces (though this also requires a political judgment by the military leadership), but militaries or officers that take matters of governance into their own hands. Healthy and proper civil-military relations arise from healthy and proper social, economic, and political relations in the society; they are neither the cause of these, nor the cure if these are absent.

It turns out that militaries and military ethics cannot safeguard democracy; only the public can do that. At best, we can encourage a model of professionalization and civil-military relations that urges members of militaries to stay out of struggles over political legitimacy, but it's nearly impossible to determine a priori how to know when political struggles have crossed the line from illegitimate struggle against a legitimate system to legitimate struggle against an illegitimate system. Nor is it realistic or even necessarily desirable to expect members of the military to maintain enough social distance from the general public that they are not affected by whatever tensions the general public is struggling with.

Augustine's fundamental hierarchicalism and simplified view of political organization, and Huntington's disdain for liberal concepts of individual values, cannot provide solutions for peoples who wrestle with the concepts of legitimacy and justice. For militaries and military service-members to do what is right, they must live in a society that expects them to do right, but that also strives to do right, itself.

REFERENCES

Albrecht, Holger (2015), "The Myth of Coup-Proofing: Risk and Instances of Military Coups d'état in the Middle East and North Africa, 1950–2013," *Armed Forces and Society* 41(4): 659–87.

Albrecht, Holger, and Deborah Ohl (2016), "Exit, Resistance, Loyalty: Military Behavior during Unrest in Authoritarian Regimes," *Perspectives on Politics* 14(1): 38–52.

Alexander, Gerard (2002), *The Sources of Democratic Consolidation*, Ithaca, NY: Cornell University Press.

Augustine (1887), *Contra Faustum*, trans. Richard Stothert, in Philip Schaff (ed.), *Nicene and Post-Nicene Fathers*, First Series, Vol. 4, Buffalo, NY: Christian Literature Publishing (rev. and ed. Kevin Knight for New Advent). Available at https://www.logicmuseum.com/wiki/Authors/Augustine, accessed April 15, 2024.

Augustine (1887), *De Mendacio*, trans. H. Browne, in Philip Schaff (ed.), *Nicene and Post-Nicene Fathers*, First Series, Vol. 3, Buffalo, NY: Christian Literature Publishing (rev. and ed. Kevin Knight for New Advent). Available at https://www.logicmuseum.com/wiki/Authors/Augustine, accessed April 15, 2024.

Augustine (1887), *De Natura Boni*, trans. Albert H. Newman, in Philip Schaff (ed.), *Nicene and Post-Nicene Fathers*, First Series, Vol. 4, Buffalo, NY: Christian Literature Publishing (rev. and ed. Kevin Knight for New Advent). Available at https://www.logicmuseum.com/wiki/Authors/Augustine, accessed April 15, 2024.

Augustine (1887), "Letter (138) to Marcellinus," trans. J. G. Cunningham, in Philip Schaff (ed.), *Nicene and Post-Nicene Fathers*, First Series, Vol. 1, Buffalo, NY: Christian Literature Publishing (rev. and ed. Kevin Knight for New Advent). Available at https://www.logicmuseum.com/wiki/Authors/Augustine, accessed April 15, 2024.

Augustine (1887), "Letter (189) to Boniface," trans. J. G. Cunningham, in Philip Schaff (ed.), *Nicene and Post-Nicene Fathers*, First Series, Vol. 3, Buffalo, NY: Christian Literature Publishing (rev. and ed. Kevin Knight for New Advent). Available at https://www.newadvent.org/fathers/1102.htm, accessed April 15, 2024.

Augustine (1888), *De Sermone Domini Monte*, trans. William Findlay, in Philip Schaff (ed.), *Nicene and Post-Nicene Fathers*, First Series, Vol. 6, Buffalo, NY: Christian Literature Publishing (rev. and ed. Kevin Knight for New Advent). Available at https://www.logicmuseum.com/wiki/Authors/Augustine, accessed April 15, 2024.

Augustine (1955), *De Libero Arbitrio*, trans. Dom Mark Pontifex, London: Longmans, Green. Available at https://www.logicmuseum.com/wiki/Authors/Augustine.

Augustine ([440] 1998), *The City of God against the Pagans*, trans. R. W. Dyson, Cambridge: Cambridge University Press.

Barany, Zoltan (2012), *The Soldier and the Changing State: Building Democratic Armies in Africa, Asia, Europe, and the Americas*, Princeton: Princeton University Press.

Barany, Zoltan (2016), *How Armies Respond to Revolutions and Why*, Princeton: Princeton University Press.

Belkin, Aaron, and Evan Schofer (2003), "Toward a Structural Understanding of Coup Risk," *Journal of Conflict Resolution* 47(5): 594–620.

Bell, Curtis (2016), "Coup d'état and Democracy," *Comparative Political Studies* 49(9): 1167–200.

Bellin, Eva (2012), "Reconsidering the Robustness of Authoritarianism in the Middle East: Lessons from the Arab Spring," *Comparative Politics* 44(2): 127–49.

Benhabib, Seyla (ed.) (1996a), *Democracy and Difference: Contesting the Boundaries of the Political*, Princeton: Princeton University Press.

Benhabib, Seyla (1996b), "Toward a Deliberative Model of Democratic Legitimacy," in Seyla Benhabib (ed.), *Democracy and Difference*, 67–94, Princeton: Princeton University Press.

Bernzen, Enno, Dirk Peddinghaus, and Robert Sieger (2016), "Innere Fuehrung: Leadership Culture in Camouflage," *Ethics and Armed Forces*, Zentrum Innere Führung. Available at ethikundmilitaer.de.

Betts, Richard K. (1977), *Soldiers, Statesmen, and Cold War Crises*, Cambridge, MA: Harvard University Press.

Bodea, Cristina, Ibrahim Elbadawi, and Christian Houle (2017), "Do Civil Wars, Coups, and Riots Have the Same Structural Determinants?," *International Interactions* 43(3): 537–61.

Böhmelt, Tobias, and Ulrich Pilster (2015), "The Impact of Institutional Coup-Proofing on Coup Attempts and Coup Outcomes," *International Interactions* 41(1): 158–82.

Bove, Vincenzo, Mauricio Rivero, and Chiara Ruffa (2020), "Beyond Coups: Terrorism and Military Involvement in Politics," *European Journal of International Relations* 26(1): 263–88.

Brooks, Risa (2013), "Abandoned at the Palace: Why the Tunisian Military Defected from the Ben Ali Regime in January 2011," *Journal of Strategic Studies* 36(2): 205–20.

Brooks, Risa (2020), "Paradoxes of Professionalism: Rethinking Civil-Military Relations in the United States," *International Security* 44(4): 7–44.

Brooks, Risa (2022), "Beyond Defection: Explaining the Tunisian and Egyptian Militaries' Divergent Roles in the Arab Spring," *Journal of Strategic Studies* 47(2): 288–315.

Burk, James (2002), "Theories of Democratic Civil-Military Relations," *Armed Forces and Society* 29(1): 7–29.

Center for the Army Profession and Ethic (2014), *The Army Ethic White Paper*. US Army TRADOC.

Chenoweth, Erica, and Maria J. Stephan (2011), *Why Civil Resistance Works: The Strategic Logic of Non-violent Conflict*, New York: Columbia University Press.

Chiozza, Giacomo, and Lena Khalifa (2023), "The Harsh Face of the Empire by Invitation: Coups in the US World Order," *Conflict Management and Peace Science* 41(2): 110–31.

Cohen, Eliot A. (2001), "The Unequal Dialogue: The Theory and Reality of Civil-Military Relations and the Use of Force," in P. Feaver and R. H. Kohn (eds.), *Soldiers and Civilians: The Civil-military Gap and American National Security*, 429–58, Cambridge: MIT Press.

Cohen, Eliot A. (2002), *Supreme Command: Soldiers, Statesmen and Leadership in Wartime*, New York: Simon and Schuster.

Cohen, Joshua (1996), "Procedure and Substance in Deliberative Democracy," in Benhabib (ed.), *Democracy and Difference*, 95–119, Princeton: Princeton University Press.

Cohn, Lindsay P. (2011), "It Wasn't in My Contract: Security Privatization and Civilian Control," *Armed Forces and Society* 37(3): 381–98.

Cohn, Lindsay P. (2018), "Political Realism and Civil-Military Relations," in Miles Hollingworth and Robert Schuett (eds.), *The Edinburgh Companion to Political Realism*, 72–84, Edinburgh: Edinburgh University Press.

Cohn, Lindsay P. (2022), "To Execute the Laws of the Union: Domestic Use of Federal Military Force in the United States," in P. Collins and R. Arcala-Hall (eds.), *Military Operation and Engagement in the Domestic Jurisdiction: Comparative Call-out Laws*, 57–90, Leiden: Brill-Nijhoff.

Collier, Paul (2008), "Let Us Now Praise Coups," *Washington Post*, June 22.

Cottey, Andrew, Timothy Edmunds, and Anthony Forster (2002), "The Second Generation Problematic: Rethinking Democracy and Civil-Military Relations," *Armed Forces and Society* 29(1): 31–56.

Crawford, Neta C. (2003), "Just War Theory and the U.S. Counterterror War," *Perspectives on Politics* 1(1): 5–25.

Croissant, Aurel, David Kuehn, Paul Chambers, and Siegfried O. Wolf (2010), "Beyond the Fallacy of Coup-ism: Conceptualizing Civilian Control of the Military in Emerging Democracies," *Democratization* 17(5): 950–75.

Croissant, Aurel, David Kuehn, and Tanja Eshenauer (2018), "Mass Protests and the Military," *Journal of Democracy* 29: 141.

Dahl, Robert A. (1956), *A Preface to Democratic Theory*, Chicago: University of Chicago Press.

Dahl, Robert A. (1989), *Democracy and Its Critics*, New Haven: Yale University Press.

Dempsey, Martin E. (2010), "America's Military—A Profession of Arms White Paper," Fort Myer, VA: US Army Training and Doctrine Command.

Derpanopoulos, George, Erica Frantz, and Barbara Geddes (2016), "Are Coups Good for Democracy?," *Research and Politics* 3(1): 1–7.

Desch, Michael C. (2001), *Civilian Control of the Military: The Changing Security Environment*, Baltimore: Johns Hopkins University Press.

Diamond, Larry (2008), "The Democratic Rollback: The Resurgence of the Predatory State," *Foreign Affairs* 87: 36–48.

Diamond, Larry (2021), "Democratic Regression in Comparative Perspective: Scope, Methods, and Causes," *Democratization* 28(1): 22–42.

Dörfler-Dierken, Angela (2005), *Ethische Fundamente der Inneren Führung*, Strausberg: Sozialwissenschaftliches Institut der Bundeswehr.

Dyson, R. W. (1998), "Introduction," in Dyson (trans. and ed.), *The City of God against the Pagans*, x–xxix, Cambridge: Cambridge University Press.

Feaver, Peter D. (1996), "The Civil-Military Problematique: Huntington, Janowitz, and the Question of Civilian Control," *Armed Forces and Society* 23(2): 149–78.

Feaver, Peter (2003), *Armed Servants: Agency, Oversight, and Civil-Military Relations*, Cambridge, MA: Harvard University Press.

Finer, Samuel (1962), *The Man on Horseback: The Role of the Military in Politics*, New Brunswick: Transaction Publishers.

Fitch, J. Samuel (1998), *The Armed Forces and Democracy in Latin America*, Baltimore: Johns Hopkins University Press.

Frantz, E., and A. Kendall-Taylor (2014), "A Dictator's Toolkit: Understanding How Co-optation Affects Repression in Autocracies," *Journal of Peace Research* 51(3): 332–46.

French, Shannon E. (2017), *The Code of the Warrior: Exploring Warrior Values Past and Present*, Lanham, MD: Rowman and Littlefield.

Geddes, Barbara (1999), "What Do We Know about Democratization after Twenty Years?," *Annual Review of Political Science* 2: 115–44.

Greenwood, Ernest (1957), "Attributes of a profession," *Social Work* 2(3): 45–55.

Habermas, Juergen (1996), "Three Normative Models of Democracy," in Benhabib (ed.), *Democracy and Difference*, 21–30, Princeton: Princeton University Press.

Hartle, Anthony E. (2004), *Moral Issues in Military Decision Making*, 2nd ed., Lawrence: Kansas University Press.

Hartman, Uwe (2016), "What's the Matter with *Innere Fuehrung*?," *Ethics and Armed Forces* 1: 22–6.

Hett, Benjamin Carter (2018), *The Death of Democracy: Hitler's Rise to Power and the Downfall of the Weimar Republic*, New York: Henry Holt.

Hughes, Whitney (2022), "National Guard Provides Critical Election Cybersecurity," *National Guard News* (Nov. 7). Available at https://www.army.mil/article/261803/national_guard_provides_critical_election_cybersecurity, accessed April 15, 2024.

Huntington, Samuel P. (1957), *The Soldier and the State: The Theory and Politics of Civil-Military Relations*, Cambridge, MA: Belknap Press of Harvard University Press.

Ingesson, Tony (2018), "When the Military Profession Isn't," in Nathan Finney and Tyrell Mayfield (eds.), *Redefining the Modern Military: The Intersection of Profession and Ethics*, 70–85, Annapolis: Naval Institute Press.

Inglehart, Ronald, and Pippa Norris (2016), "Trump, Brexit, and the Rise of Populism: Economic Have-Nots and Cultural Backlash," *Harvard Faculty Research Working Paper Series* RWP16-026.

Janowitz, Morris (1960), *The Professional Soldier: A Social and Political Portrait*, New York: Free Press.

Jenne, Nicole, and Rafael Martínez (2022), "Domestic Military Missions in Latin America: Civil-Military Relations and the Perpetuation of Democratic Deficits," *European Journal of International Security* 7(1): 58–83.

Johnson, Thomas H., Robert O. Slater, and Pat McGowan (1984), "Explaining African Military Coups d'Etat, 1960–1982," *American Political Science Review* 78(3): 622–40.

Kamrava, Mehran (2000), "Military Professionalization and Civil-Military Relations in the Middle East," *Political Science Quarterly* 115(1): 67–92.

Kant, Immanuel ([1797] 2017), "The Doctrine of Right," in Lara Denis (ed.) and Mary Gregor (trans.), *The Metaphysics of Morals*, 1–148, Cambridge: Cambridge University Press.

Kenwick, Michael (2020), "Self-Reinforcing Civilian Control: A Measurement-Based Analysis of Civil-Military Relations," *International Studies Quarterly* 64: 71–84.

Kieh, George K., and Pita O. Agbese (eds.) (2005), *The Military and Politics in Africa: From Engagement to Democratic and Constitutional Control*, Farnham: Ashgate Press.

Krebs, Ronald, Robert Ralston, and Aaron Rapport (2023), "No Right to Be Wrong: What Americans Think about Civil-Military Relations," *Perspectives on Politics* 21(2): 606–24.

Kuehn, David (2017), "Midwives or Gravediggers of Democracy? The Military's Impact on Democratic Development," *Democratization* 24(5): 783–800.

Kyle, Brett J., and Andrew G. Reiter (2021), *Military Courts, Civil-Military Relations, and the Legal Battle for Democracy*, New York: Routledge.

Langan, John (1984), "The Elements of St. Augustine's Just War Theory," *Journal of Religious Ethics* 12(1): 19–38.

Lee, Terence (2005), "Military Cohesion and Regime Maintenance: Explaining the Role of the Military in 1989 China and 1998 Indonesia," *Armed Forces & Society* 32(1): 80–104.

Lee, Terence (2015), *Defect or Defend: Military Responses to Popular Protests in Authoritarian Asia*, Baltimore: Johns Hopkins University Press.

Levitsky, Steven, and Daniel Ziblatt (2019), *How Democracies Die*, New York: Crown.

Lijphart, Arend (1999), *Patterns of Democracy: Government Forms and Performance in Thirty-Six Countries*, New Haven: Yale University Press.

Linz, Juan (1990), "The Perils of Presidentialism," *Journal of Democracy* 1: 51–70.

Linz, Juan, and Alfred Stepan (eds.) (1978), *The Breakdown of Democratic Regimes*, Baltimore: Johns Hopkins University Press.

Locke, John ([1689] 1999), "The Second Treatise on Civil Government," in Robert C. Cummins and Thomas D. Christiano (eds.), *Modern Moral and Political Philosophy*, 117–74, London: Mayfield.
Londregan, John B., and Keith T. Poole (1990), "Poverty, the Coup Trap, and the Seizure of Executive Power," *World Politics* 42(2): 151–83.
MacIntyre, Alasdair C. (2015), "Military Ethics: A Discipline in Crisis," in George Lucas (ed.), *Routledge Handbook of Military Ethics*, 3–14, Abington, Oxon: Routledge.
Madison, James ([1787] 1961), *The Federalist Papers*, Clinton Rossiter (ed.), New York: Mentor.
Makara, Michael (2013), "Coup-Proofing, Military Defection, and the Arab Spring," *Democracy and Security* 9: 334–59.
Mansbridge, Jane (1996), "Using Power/Fighting Power: The Polity," in Benhabib (ed.), *Democracy and Difference*, 46–66, Princeton: Princeton University Press.
Marinov, Nikolay, and Hein Goemans (2014), "Coups and Democracy," *British Journal of Political Science* 44(4): 799–825.
McLauchlin, Theo (2010), "Loyalty Strategies and Military Defection in Rebellion," *Comparative Politics* 42(3): 333–50.
Mill, John Stuart ([1859] 1978), *On Liberty*, Indianapolis: Hackett Publishing.
Moten, Matthew (2010), "The Army Officers' Professional Ethic: Past, Present, and Future," Vol. 2, Carlisle, PA: Strategic Studies Institute.
Nordlinger, Eric A. (1977), *Soldiers in Politics: Military Coups and Governments*, Englewood Cliffs, NJ: Prentice Hall.
Parsons, Talcott (1937), "Remarks on Education and the Professions," *International Journal of Ethics* 47(3): 365–69.
Parsons, Talcott (1939), "The Professions and Social Functions through a Network of Formal and Structure," *Social Forces* 17: 457–67.
Petty, Keith A. (2018), "Duty and Disobedience: the conflict of conscience and compliance in the Trump era," *Pepperdine Law Review* 45(1): 55–148.
Pion-Berlin, David, and Harold Trinkunas (2005), "Democratization, Social Crisis, and the Impact of Military Domestic Roles in Latin America," *Journal of Political and Military Sociology* 33(1): 5–24.
Pion-Berlin, David, Diego Esparza, and Kevin Grisham (2014), "Staying Quartered: Civilian Uprisings and Military Disobedience in the Twenty-First Century," *Comparative Political Studies* 47(2): 230–59.
Plato ([n.d.] 1968), *The Republic*, Allan Bloom (trans.), New York: Basic Books.
Powell, Jonathan, Christopher Faulkner, William Dean, and Kyle Romano (2018), "Give Them Toys? Military Allocations and Regime Stability in Transitional Democracies," *Democratization* 25(7): 1153–72.

Przeworski, Adam (1991), *Democracy and the Market: Political and Economic Reforms in Eastern Europe and Latin America*, Cambridge: Cambridge University Press.

Quinlivan, James T. (1999), "Coup-Proofing: Its Practice and Consequences in the Middle East," *International Security* 24: 131–65.

Rawls, John (2001), *Justice as Fairness: A Restatement*, Cambridge, MA: Belknap Press of Harvard University Press.

Robinson, Michael A., Lindsay P. Cohn, and Max Z. Margulies (2021), "Dissents and Sensibility: Conflicting Loyalties, Democracy, and Civil-Military Relations," in Lionel Beehner, Risa Brooks, and Daniel Maurer (eds.), *Reconsidering American Civil-Military Relations: The Military, Society, Politics, and Modern War*, 63–81, Oxford: Oxford University Press.

Rousseau, Jean-Jacques ([1755] 1999), "*Discourse on Inequality*," in Robert C. Cummins and Thomas D. Christiano (eds.), *Modern Moral and Political Philosophy*, 412–45, London: Mayfield.

Rousseau, Jean-Jacques ([1762] 1999), "*The Social Contract*," in Robert C. Cummins and Thomas D. Christiano (eds.), *Modern Moral and Political Philosophy*, 357–411, London: Mayfield.

Ryfe, David M. (2005), "Does Deliberative Democracy Work?," *Annual Review of Political Science* 8: 49–71.

Saks, Mike (2012), "Defining a Profession: The Role of Knowledge and Expertise," *Professions and Professionalism* 2(1): 1–10.

Sarkesian, Samuel C. (1981), "Military Professionalism and Civil-Military Relations in the West," *International Political Science Review* 2(3): 283–97.

Schelling, Thomas (1966), *Arms and Influence*, New Haven: Yale University Press.

Schumpeter, Joseph A. ([1942] 2008), *Capitalism, Socialism, and Democracy*, New York: Harper Perennial.

Shanks Kaurin, Pauline (2018a), "Ethics: Starting at the Beginning," *WavellRoom* (Aug. 23). Available at https://wavellroom.com/2018/08/23/ethics-starting-beginning/, accessed April 15, 2024.

Shanks Kaurin, Pauline (2018b), "Questioning Military Professionalism," in Nathan K. Finney and Tyrell O. Mayfield (eds.), *Redefining the Modern Military: The Intersection of Profession and Ethics*, 9–21, Annapolis, MD: Naval Institute Press.

Shanks Kaurin, Pauline (2020), *On Obedience: Contrasting Philosophies for the Military, Citizenry, and Community*, Annapolis, MD: Naval Institute Press.

Singh, Naunihal (2014), *Seizing Power: The Strategic Logic of Military Coups*, Baltimore: Johns Hopkins University Press.

Snider, Don M. (2014), "Renewing the Motivational Power of the Army's Professional Ethic," *Parameters* 44(3): 7–11.
Snider, Don M. (2015), "American Military Professions and Their Ethics," in George Lucas (ed.), *Routledge Handbook of Military Ethics*, 15–31, Abingdon, Oxon: Routledge.
Spreitzer, G. M., and Sonenshein, S. (2003), "Positive Deviance and Extraordinary Organizing," in K. Cameron, J. Dutton, and R. Quinn (eds.), *Positive Organizational Scholarship*, 207–24, San Francisco: Berrett-Koehler.
Stepan, Alfred (1986), "Paths toward Redemocratization," in Laurence Whitehead, Philippe C. Schmitter, and Guillermo A. O'Donnell (eds.), *Transitions from Authoritarian Rule: Comparative Perspectives*, 64–84, Baltimore: Johns Hopkins University Press.
Stepan, Alfred (1988), *Rethinking Military Politics: Brazil and the Southern Cone*, Princeton, NJ: Princeton University Press.
Sudduth, J. K. (2017), "Coup Risk, Coup-Proofing, and Leader Survival," *Journal of Peace Research* 54(1): 3–15.
Svolik, Milan W. (2015), "Which Democracies Will Last? Coups, Incumbent Takeovers, and the Dynamic of Democratic Consolidation," *British Journal of Political Science* 45(4): 715–38.
Swain, Richard M., and Albert C. Pierce (2017), *The Armed Forces Officer*, Washington, DC: NDU Press.
Talmadge, Caitlin (2015), *The Dictator's Army: Battlefield Effectiveness in Authoritarian Regimes*, Ithaca, NY: Cornell University Press.
Tansey, Oisin (2016), "The Limits of the 'Democratic Coup' Thesis: International Politics and Post-Coup Authoritarianism," *Journal of Global Security Studies* 1(3): 220–34.
Thyne, Clayton L., and Jonathan M. Powell (2016), "Coup d'état or Coup d'Autocracy? How Coups Impact Democratization, 1950–2008," *Foreign Policy Analysis* 12(2): 192–213.
Thyne, Clayton L., and Jonathan M. Powell (2019), "Coup Research," in *Oxford Research Encyclopedia of International Studies*, Oxford: Oxford University Press.
Tyler, Tom R. (1990), *Why People Obey the Law*, New Haven: Yale University Press.
US Army Regulation 600–100, *Army Profession and Leadership Policy*, HQ Department of the Army (5 Apr 2017) ARN3758_AR_600–100_FINAL_WEB_.pdf (army.mil).
Vadera, Abhijeet K., Michael G. Pratt, and Pooja Mishra (2013), "Constructive Deviance in Organizations: Integrating and Moving Forward," *Journal of Management* 39(5): 1221–76.
Walzer, Michael (2002), "The Triumph of Just War Theory (and the Dangers of Success)," *Social Research* 69(4): 925–44.

White, Peter (2023), "Getting a Seat at the Table: Changes in Military Participation in Government and Coups," *Research & Politics* 10(1): online first.
Wilensky, Harold L. (1964), "The Professionalization of Everyone?," *American Journal of Sociology* 70(2): 137–58.
Williams, Robert E., and Dan Caldwell (2006), "Jus Post Bellum: Just War Theory and the Principles of Just Peace," *International Studies Perspectives* 7: 309–20.
Wolin, Sheldon (1996), "Fugitive Democracy," in Benhabib (ed.), *Democracy and Difference*, 31–45, Princeton: Princeton University Press.
Wynn, Phillip (2013), *Augustine on War and Military Service*, Minneapolis: Fortress Press.
Young, Iris Marion (1996), "Communication and the Other: Beyond Deliberative Democracy," in Benhabib (ed.), *Democracy and Difference*, 120–35, Princeton: Princeton University Press.

INDEX

Arab Spring 2, 3, 60

Burk, James 52, 56

Clausewitz, Carl von 81–2
Cohen, Eliot 1, 5, 55, 66–7, 85

Dahl, Robert 28, 30–1
democratic coup 59
Diamond, Larry 64–5

Feaver, Peter 5, 20, 51, 62, 65, 72, 87
Finer, Samuel 58, 60, 62

Habermas, Juergen 28–30, 35–6, 42–5
Huntington, Samuel 1–5, 8, 21–5, 28, 51–2, 55–6, 62, 66–8, 72–4, 78, 84–5, 91

Janowitz, Morris 52, 56, 66, 68, 73–4, 85
Just War 6, 17

Kant, Immanuel 1, 29–30

legitimization of violence 6–8, 13–18, 28, 32, 38, 46, 66, 82–4
Linz, Juan 50, 58, 63–4
Locke, John 27, 29, 31–5, 38

MacIntyre, Alasdair 87–8
Madison, James 31, 38, 40, 46–7
military professionalism 2, 4, 51, 68, 71
Mill, John Stuart 31, 34–5

Plato 4, 12, 18, 27, 35
professional ethics 3, 6, 8, 49–61, 68, 70–82, 86–7, 90
professionalism 1, 3–4, 51–8, 68, 72, 74, 78

Rousseau, Jean-Jacques 30, 34–40

Sarkesian, Samuel 4, 52–3, 55, 66–7, 85
Schumpeter, Joseph 28–30
soldier's role in politics
    soldier as advisor 19, 20, 33, 41, 45, 67, 83–4
    soldier as citizen 19, 22, 33–4, 42, 45, 68, 83–5
    soldier as enforcer 21–2, 34, 41, 45, 67, 83–5
    soldier as politician 19–21, 33–4, 40, 45, 66, 83–4
Stepan, Alfred 5, 51, 53–4, 57–8, 65–6

Trump, Donald 1, 3, 5